A FIERY FLAME

A FIERY FLAME

Encountering God's Word

James H. Kroeger

Joseph D. Zaldivar

Editors

Claretian
Publications

Insta
Publications

Jesuit
Communications

A FIERY FLAME
Encountering God's Word

Claretian Publications is a pastoral endeavor of the Claretian Missionaries in the Philippines.

Claretian Communications Foundation, Inc.
U.P.P.O. Box 4, Diliman 1101 Quezon City, Philippines
Tel: 921-3984 • Fax: 921-6205
cci@claret.org • www.claretianpublications.com

Insta Publications is a collaborative effort of the alumni association and student body of San Jose Major Seminary, Quezon City, Philippines.

Insta Publications of San Jose Seminary
U.P.P.O. Box 237, Diliman 1144 Quezon City, Philippines
Tel: 426-6091 • Fax: 426-5936 • insta@josefino.net

Jesuit Communications produces audio-visual and print media for evangelization and education.

Jesuit Communications Foundation, Inc.
Sonolux Building – Ateneo de Manila University
Loyola Heights, Quezon City, Philippines
Tel: 426-5971 to 72 • Fax: 426-5970
jcf@admu.edu.ph • www.ignaciana.org/jescom

Library of Congress Cataloguing-in-Publication Data

Kroeger, James H. / Zaldivar, Joseph D.
    A FIERY FLAME
        Encountering God's Word
        p. xii + 119   cm. 15.24 x 22.86
        ISBN 978-971-0511-56-3

    1. Bible—Hermeneutics. 2. Bible—Use. 3. Catholic Church—Doctrines. I. Kroeger, James H. II. Zaldivar, Joseph D. III. Arévalo, Catalino G. IV. Bacani, Teodoro C. V. David, Pablo V. VI. Tagle, Luis A. VII. Title.
        BS 476.F54 2010
        220.6—dc22

CONTENTS

PREFACE

The Good Book contains the story of three characters who "ate" the word of God. One is the prophet Jeremiah who, when he found God's words, ate them, and they became for him the delight of his heart (Jer 15:16). This was quite the same experience of the prophet Ezekiel, who during a magnificent vision, was commanded to eat a scroll that contained lamentation and mourning (Ezek 2:8-3:3). For both prophets, "eating God's word" became a happy experience, because it was in their mouths "sweet as honey." In the New Testament, John of Patmos, like Ezekiel, had a vision wherein he was commanded to eat a scroll (Rev 10:8-10). Like the prophets, John found the scroll to be honey-sweet for his mouth; however, unlike the prophets, he reports further that it soured his stomach.

The Church does not just hand on the Word, proclaiming it to the ends of the earth. Like the prophets, before one can preach the Word, one must receive it first, listen to it intently, and eat it. To "eat" God's word is an excellent image for how Christians should receive the Word. The Word is not just read or studied like required texts in an academic course; rather, it must be chewed, swallowed, digested; it becomes part of the individual. To receive the Word, the whole person—body and soul, giftedness and brokenness—and the whole community—clergy and laity, rich and poor, sinner and saint—are engaged in listening to it intently. God's word transforms, nourishes, gives life, and empowers the recipient *in opus ministerii* (in the work of ministry).

Like the author of the Apocalypse, disciples must let the Word break them and come into the stomach, often bringing bitterness. Brokenness is necessary for the *Verbum* to touch our *caro* (flesh); human brokenness allows the Word to consume the person. Thus, the Word is not just a part of the individual; the person becomes part of the Word. The Church that *houses the fire* of the Word must constantly be challenged and changed by it, even if this means embracing painful realities and difficult ideals. Only then can Christ's disciples rightfully traverse the *missionary roads* of the Word and echo its creative and transformative *voice* so that its *Face* may be seen *insta opportune, importune* (whether welcome or unwelcome).

Truly, the undersigned is honored to introduce this book which collects the presentations made during the *Josefino Forum: Verbum Dei* held on October 4, 2009. These are reflections from distinguished leaders and teachers in the Philippine Church; they are focused on the Word of God in the life and mission of the Church. The presenters share how they themselves have "eaten" the Word and how it indeed has become for them sweet as honey in their mouths, but also often bitter in their stomachs. They invite Jesus' disciples to partake of the nourishing Word; disciples expect to be empowered and yet broken, just as a fiery flame can make one glow and shine but, at the same time, that very flame can char and burn.

Joseph D. Zaldivar
Insta Editor

INTRODUCTION

"Ignorance of the Scriptures is ignorance of Christ." In these succinct words, Saint Jerome, great biblical scholar and translator, captured the pivotal importance for all Christians of a depth knowledge of sacred scripture. Jerome's words were quoted by the Second Vatican Council in its document on revelation (*Dei Verbum* 25); Vatican II affirmed that it is only through frequent reading of the divine scriptures that believers will come to the "excelling knowledge of Jesus Christ" (Phil 3:8).

More than four decades after the close of the Council, the Church recently held the Twelfth Ordinary General Assembly of the Synod of Bishops; it took place in Rome on October 5-26, 2008, with the theme: "The Word of God in the Life and Mission of the Church." By all accounts, this Synod was a concerted effort on the part of the Church to place a new and vibrant emphasis on the Word, especially in the Bible. Bishop Michael Putney of Australia noted: "This was the reception of *Dei Verbum* in the heart of the Church."

The Twelfth Synod of Bishops was a massive undertaking. Two hundred and fifty-three members representing one hundred and thirteen bishops' conferences were in attendance. The Synod was assisted by thirty-nine biblical experts. Thirty-seven guests were invited as well as ten non-Catholic religious leaders. Pope Benedict XVI was present for most of the twice-daily sessions and even commented on the topic of biblical exegesis. The opening

Eucharistic celebration was held in the Basilica of Saint Paul Outside the Walls, recognizing that the Church was in the midst of the celebration of the Year of Saint Paul.

The World Synod of Bishops, emerging anew from discussions at Vatican II, employs a rather elaborate and comprehensive process for each of its sessions, usually held once every three years [the previous synod, held in 2005, focused on the Eucharist]. The Synod process begins with a *Lineamenta* (guidelines and questions) sent to bishops to elicit their suggestions. From these the *Instrumentum Laboris* (working document) is drafted. At the first session of the Synod, the *Relatio* (pre-discussion report) is given by the General Reporter. The next weeks bring a wide variety of input, discussion, exchanges and recommendations. At the close of the proceedings, a *Nuntius* or "Message to the People of God" is released; a final concelebrated Eucharist concludes the Synod. Within a year or two, the pope normally responds with an apostolic exhortation on the theme of the synod.

The *Nuntius* or Message from a Synod is generally quite brief; however, the *Nuntius* of the 2008 Synod proved to be an exception, reaching over twenty pages. The first section of this book reproduces the full text of the *Nuntius* or Synod Message. It is a well-crafted document, rich in content and filled with insightful reflections. It has four parts; each part is headed by an aspect of the Word of God. The four phases are: Voice, Face, House, and Roads of the Word of God.

Part One bears the title: *The Voice of the Word: Revelation.* It presents the Word of God itself as divine revelation in which God speaks to humanity and reveals himself; Bishop Tagle elaborates on this theme. Part Two is entitled: *The Face of the Word: Jesus Christ.* In Jesus of Nazareth the Word of God becomes human; Father Arévalo offers some reflection on this section, found within his final overview-synthesis. Part Three elaborates *The House of the Word: The Church;* Bishop David offers his insights on this theme. Finally, Part Four, entitled *The Roads of the Word: Mission,* focuses on the evangelizing mission of the Church; reflections and challenges are offered by Bishop Bacani.

The final concluding section of the *Nuntius* urges all to read and study the Bible: "Brothers and sisters of the whole world, let us receive this invitation; let us approach the table of the word of God, so as to be nourished and live 'not on bread alone but on every word that comes from the mouth of God'." Indeed, God's word is "sweeter than honey"; it is "a fire" and "a lamp for my feet"; it is like "rain that irrigates the earth." A word of encouragement concludes the Synodal Message: "Let us now remain silent, to hear the word of God with effectiveness and let us maintain this silence after hearing, so that it may continue to dwell in us, to live in us, and to speak to us."

Pope Benedict XVI concluded the Synod with a concelebrated Mass in Saint Peter's Basilica. In his homily, he noted: "All of us who have taken part in the work of the Synod will carry with us the renewed knowledge that the Church's principal task at the start of this new millennium is above all to nourish ourselves with the Word of God, in order to make more effective the pledge of the new evangelization, the announcement of our times."

Finally, the pope offered a prayer: "Most Holy Mary, who offered your life up as the 'servant of the Lord' so that everything would happen in accordance with the divine will (cf. Lk 1:38) and who told us to do whatever Jesus tells us to do (cf. Jn 2:5), teach us to recognize in our lives the primacy of the word that alone can grant salvation."

The *"Verbum Dei* Forum" held on October 4, 2009

proved to be a creative and effective avenue to bring to the Philippine context the insights of the 2008 Synod of Bishops on "The Word of God in the Life and Mission of the Church." This modest book contains all the material of the forum, conveniently assembled for further reflection and prayer. It is the fond hope of all who collaborated in this event that "as the rain and snow come down from heaven and do not return there until they have watered the earth ... so shall my word be.... It shall not return to me empty" (Is 55:10-11). We all are challenged by what we read in James: we must not be only hearers of the Word, but doers of the Word (1:19-27), for faith that does not lead to works is dead (2:14-17). Love the Word of God! Live the Word of God!

James H. Kroeger, M.M.
General Editor

Part One

Message
to the
People of God

World Synod of Bishops

Message to the People of God

World Synod of Bishops

Brothers and sisters, "May God the Father and the Lord Jesus Christ grant peace, love and faith to all the brothers. May grace be with all who love our Lord Jesus Christ, in life imperishable." With this intense and passionate greeting, Saint Paul concluded his letter to the Christians of Ephesus (6:23-24). With these same words we, the Synod Fathers, gathered in Rome for the XII Ordinary General Assembly of the Synod of Bishops, under the guidance of the Holy Father Benedict XVI, open our message addressed to the vast horizon of all those who, in the various regions of the world, follow Christ as disciples, and continue to love him with an imperishable love.

We will again propose to them the voice and the light of the word of God, repeating the ancient call: "the word is very near to you, it is in your mouth and in your heart for you to put into practice" (Deut 30:14). And God himself will say to each one: "Son of man, take to heart everything I say to you, listen carefully" (Ezek 3:10). We are about to propose a spiritual journey consisting of four phases and that will carry us from all eternity and the infinite nature of God to our homes and the streets of our cities.

I. THE VOICE OF THE WORD: REVELATION

1. "Then the Lord spoke to you from the heart of the

fire; you heard the sound of words but saw no shape; there was only a voice!" (Deut 4:12). It is Moses who speaks, evoking the experience lived by Israel in the bitter solitude of the Sinai desert. The Lord presented himself not as an image or an effigy or a statue similar to a golden calf, but with "a voice of words." It is a voice which entered the scene at the very beginning of creation, when it tore through the silence of nothingness: "In the beginning ... God said, 'Let there be light,' and there was light.... In the beginning was the Word: the Word was with God and the Word was God.... Through him all things came into being, not one thing came into being except through him" (Gen 1:1,3; John 1:1,3).

Creation is not born of a battle of divinities, as taught by ancient Mesopotamian myths, but of a word which defeats nothingness and creates being. The Psalmist sings: "By the word of the Lord the heavens were made, by the breath of his mouth all their array ... for, the moment he spoke, it was so, no sooner had he commanded, than there it stood" (Ps 33:6.9). And Saint Paul will repeat: God "brings the dead to life and calls into existence what does not yet exist" (Rom 4:17). Thus, a first "cosmic" revelation is found which makes creation similar to an immense page opened up before all of humanity, in which a message from the Creator can be read: "The heavens declare the glory of God, the vault of heaven proclaims his handiwork, day unto day makes known his message; night unto night hands on the knowledge. There is no speech or language where their voice is not heard. Their message goes out into all the earth" (Ps 19:2-5).

2. The divine word is, however, also at the origin of human history. Man and woman, whom God created "in his own image" (Gen 1:27), and who bear within themselves the divine imprint, can enter into dialogue with their Creator or can wander far from him and reject him by sinning. The word of God, then, saves and judges, penetrating the woven fabric of history with its tales and events: "I have indeed seen the misery of my people in Egypt. I have heard them crying.... I am well aware of their sufferings. And I have come down to rescue them from the clutches of the Egyptians and bring them up out of that country, to a country rich and broad" (Ex 3:7-8). The divine is therefore present in human events which, through the action of the Lord of history, are inserted in the greater plan of salvation for "everyone to be saved and reach full knowledge of the truth" (1 Tim 2:4).

3. Consequently, the effective, creative and salvific divine word is source of being and of history, of creation and redemption. The Lord encounters humanity declaring: "I, the Lord, have spoken and done this" (Ezek 37:14). The voice of God then passes into the written word, the *Graphé* or the *Graphaí*, the Sacred Scriptures, as it is said in the New Testament. Moses had already descended from the mount of Sinai, "with the two tablets of the commandments in his hands, tablets inscribed on both sides, inscribed on the front and on the back. The tablets were the work of God, and the writing on them was God's writing" (Ex 32:15-16). Moses himself obliged Israel to preserve and rewrite these "tablets of the commandments": "On these stones you must write all the words of this Law very plainly" (Deut 27:8).

The Sacred Scriptures "bear witness" to the divine word in written form. They memorialize the creative and saving event of revelation by way of canonical, historical and literary means. Therefore, the word of God precedes and goes beyond the Bible which itself is "inspired by God" and contains the efficacious divine word (cf. 2 Tim 3:16). This is why our faith is not only centered on a book, but on a history of salvation and, as we will see, on a person, Jesus Christ, the Word of God made flesh, man and history. Precisely because the capacity of the divine word embraces and extends beyond the Scripture, the constant presence of the Holy Spirit that "will lead you to the complete truth" (John 16:13) is necessary for those who read the Bible. This is the great Tradition: the effective presence of the "Spirit of truth" in the Church, guardian of Sacred Scripture, which are authentically interpreted by the Church's Magisterium. This Tradition enables the Church to understand, interpret, communicate and bear witness to the word of God. Saint Paul himself, proclaiming the first Christian creed, will recognize the need to "transmit" what he "had received" from Tradition (1 Cor 15:3-5).

II. THE FACE OF THE WORD: JESUS CHRIST

4. In the original Greek, there are only three fundamental words: *Lógos sarx eghéneto*, "the Word was made flesh." And yet, this is the summit not only of that poetic and theological jewel which is the prologue to John's Gospel (John 1:14), but it is the actual heart of the Christian faith. The eternal and divine Word enters into space and time and takes on a human face and identity, so much so that it is possible to approach him directly asking, as did the group of Greeks present in Jerusalem: "We should like to see Jesus" (John 12:20-21). Words without a face are not perfect, they do not fully complete the encounter, as Job recalled, reaching the end of his dramatic itinerary of searching: "Before, I knew you only by hearsay but now" ... I have "seen you with my own eyes" (Job 42:5).

Christ is "the Word [that] was with God and the Word was God" (John 1:1). "He is the image of the unseen God, the first-born of all creation" (Col 1:15); but he is also Jesus of Nazareth who walks the roads of a marginal province of the Roman Empire, who speaks the local language, who reveals the traits of a people, the Jews, and its culture. Therefore the real Jesus Christ is fragile and mortal flesh; he is history and humanity, but he is also glory, divinity, mystery: he who revealed God to us, the God no one has ever seen (cf. John 1:18). The Son of God continues to be so even in the dead body placed in the sepulcher and the resurrection is the living and clear proof to this fact.

5. Christian tradition has often placed the Divine Word made flesh on a parallel with the same word made book. This is what emerges already in the creed when one professes that the Son of God "was incarnate by the Holy Spirit of the Virgin Mary, and was made man," but also a profession of faith in the same "Holy Spirit, who spoke through the Prophets." The Second Vatican Council gathers this ancient tradition according to which "the body of the Son is the Scripture transmitted to us"—as Saint Ambrose affirms (*In Lucam* VI, 33)—and clearly declares: "For the words of God, expressed in human language, have been made like human discourse, just as the Word of the eternal Father, when he took to himself the flesh of human weakness, was in every way made like men" (DV 13).

Indeed, the Bible is also "flesh," "letter"; it expresses itself in particular languages, in literary and historical forms, in concepts tied to an ancient culture, it preserves the memories of events, often tragic; its pages not infrequently are marked by blood and violence, within it resounds the laughter of humanity and the flowing tears, as well as the cry of the distressed and the joy of those in love. For this, its "bodily" dimension requires an historical and literary analysis, which occurs through various methods and approaches offered by Biblical exegesis. Every reader of Sacred Scripture, even the most simple, must have a proportionate knowledge of the sacred text, recalling that the word is enveloped in concrete words, which is shaped and adapted to make it heard and understood by all of humanity. This is a necessary commitment. If it is excluded, one could fall into fundamentalism which in practice denies the Incarnation of the divine Word in history, does not recognize that this word expresses itself in the Bible according to a human language that must be decoded, studied and understood. Such an attitude ignores that divine inspiration did not erase the historical identities and personalities of its human authors. The Bible, however, is also the eternal and divine Word and for this reason requires another understanding, given by the Holy Spirit who unveils the transcendent dimensions of the divine word, present in human words.

6. Here, thus, lies the necessity of the "living Tradition of all the Church" (DV 12) and of the faith to understand Sacred Scripture in a full and unified way. Should one focus only on the "letter," the Bible is only a solemn document of the past, a noble, ethical and cultural witness. If, however, the Incarnation is excluded, it could fall into a fundamentalist equivocation or a vague spiritualism or pop-psychology. Exegetical knowledge must, therefore, weave itself indissolubly with spiritual and theological tradition so that the divine and human unity of Jesus Christ and Scripture is not broken.

In this rediscovered harmony, the face of Christ will shine in its fullness and will help us to discover another unity, that profound and intimate unity of Sacred Scriptures. There are, indeed, seventy-three books, but they form only one "Canon," in one dialogue between God and humanity, in one plan of salvation. "At many moments in the past and by many means, God spoke to our ancestors through the prophets; but in our time, the final days, he has spoken to us in the person of his Son" (Heb 1:1-2). Christ thus retrospectively sheds his light on the entire development of salvation history and reveals its coherence, meaning, and direction. He is the seal, "the Alpha and the Omega" (Rev 1:8) of a dialogue between God and his creatures distributed over time and attested to in the Bible. It is in the light of this final seal that the words of Moses and the prophets acquire their "full sense." Jesus himself had indicated this on that spring afternoon, while he made his way from Jerusalem to the town of Emmaus, dialoguing with Cleopas and his friend, explaining "to them the passages in the Scriptures that were about himself" (Luke 24:27).

That the divine Word has put on a face is at the center of Revelation. That is precisely why the ultimate finality of biblical knowledge is "not the result of an ethical choice or a lofty idea, but the encounter with an event, a person, which gives life a new horizon and a decisive direction" (*Deus caritas est* 1).

III. THE HOUSE OF THE WORD: THE CHURCH

Just as divine wisdom in the Old Testament made her house in the cities of men and women, supporting it with seven pillars (cf. Prov 9:1), thus also the word of God made its house in the New Testament. The Church has as her model the mother community of Jerusalem. The Church is founded on Peter and the apostles and today, through the bishops in communion with the Successor of Peter, continues to keep, announce and interpret the word of God (cf. LG 13). In the Acts of the Apostles (2:42), Luke traces its architecture based on four ideal pillars: "These remained faithful to the teaching of the apostles, to the brotherhood, to the breaking of bread and to the prayers."

7. Here, first of all, is the apostolic *didaché*, that is to say the preaching of the word of God. The Apostle Paul, in fact, warns us that "faith comes from hearing, and what is heard comes through the word of Christ" (Rm 10:17). The voice of the herald comes from the Church, which proposes *kérygma*, that is to say, the primary and fundamental announcement that Jesus himself had proclaimed at the beginning of his public ministry: "The time is fulfilled, and the kingdom of God is close at hand. Repent and believe the gospel" (Mark 1:15). The apostles, proclaiming the death and resurrection of Christ, announce the unveiling of the kingdom of God, that is to say, the decisive divine intervention in the history of humanity: "Only in him is there salvation; for of all the names in the world given to humanity, this is the only one by which we can be saved" (Acts 4:12). The Christian bears witness to this hope "with courtesy and respect and with a clear conscience," ready, however, to be involved and, perhaps, to be overwhelmed by the storms of refusal and persecution, knowing that "it is better to suffer for doing right than for doing wrong" (1 Pet 3:16-17).

Catechesis, then, resounds in the Church: this is destined to deepen in the Christian "the understanding of the mystery of Christ in the light of God's word, so that the whole of a person's humanity is impregnated by that word" in Christianity (John Paul II, *Catechesi tradendae* 20). But, the high point of preaching is in the homily which, for many Christians, is still today the central moment of encounter with the word of God. In this act, the minister should be transformed into a prophet as well. He, in fact, with a clear, incisive and substantial language must not only proclaim with authority "God's wonderful works in the history of salvation" (SC 35)—offered first by a clear and vivid reading of the biblical text proposed in the liturgy—but he must also act upon it in the times and moments lived by the hearers and make the question of conversion and vital commitment blossom in their hearts: "What are we to do, brothers?" (Acts 2:37).

Preaching, catechesis and the homily therefore presuppose a reading and understanding, an explaining and interpreting, an involvement of the mind and of the heart.

Thus in preaching a dual movement is achieved. With the first, one goes back to the roots of the sacred texts, the events, the first words of the history of salvation, to understand them in their meaning and in their message. With the second movement, one returns to the present, to the today lived by those who hear and read, always with Christ in mind, who is the guiding light destined to unite the Scriptures. This is what Jesus himself did—as has already been said—in his journey to Jerusalem in Emmaus with two of his disciples. This is what the deacon Phillip would do on the way from Jerusalem to Gaza, when he spoke this emblematic dialogue with the Ethiopian official: "Do you understand what you are reading? … How could I, unless I have someone to guide me?" (Acts 8:30-31). And the finality will be the full encounter with Christ in the sacrament. This is how the second pillar that supports the Church, the house of the divine word, presents itself.

8. It is in the breaking of the bread. The scene at Emmaus (cf. Luke 24:13-35) is once again exemplary, and reproduces what happens every day in our churches: the homily by Jesus about Moses and the prophets gives way to the breaking of the Eucharistic Bread at the table. This is the moment of God's intimate dialogue with His people. It is the act of the new covenant sealed in the blood of Christ (cf. Luke 22:20). It is the supreme work of the Word who offers himself as food in his immolated body, it is the source and summit of the life and mission of the Church. The Gospel account of the Last Supper, the memorial of Christ's sacrifice, when proclaimed in the Eucharistic celebration, through the invocation of the Holy Spirit, becomes event and sacrament. This is why the Second Vatican Council, in a very intense passage, declared: "The Church has always venerated the divine Scriptures just as she venerates the body of the Lord, since, especially in the sacred liturgy, she unceasingly receives and offers to the faithful the bread of life from the table both of God's word and of Christ's body" (DV 21). Therefore, we must place at the center of Christian life "the liturgy of the word and the Eucharistic liturgy, [which] are so closely connected with each other that they form but one single act of worship" (SC 56).

9. The third pillar of the spiritual building of the Church, the house of the word, is made up of prayers, woven from—as recalled by Saint Paul—"psalms and hymns and inspired songs" (Col 3:16). A privileged place is naturally taken by the Liturgy of the Hours, the prayer of the Church *par excellence,* destined to give rhythm to the days and times of the Christian year, offering, above all with the Psalmody, the daily spiritual food of the faithful. Alongside this and the community celebrations of the word, tradition has introduced the practice of *Lectio divina,* the prayerful reading in the Holy Spirit that is able to open to the faithful the treasure of the word of God, and also to create the encounter with Christ, the living divine Word.

This begins with the reading (*lectio*) of the text, which provokes the question of true knowledge of its real content: what does the biblical text say in itself? Then follows meditation (*meditatio*) where the question is: what does the Biblical text say to us? In this manner, one arrives at prayer (*oratio*), which presupposes this other question: what do we say to the Lord in answer to his word? And one ends with contemplation (*contemplatio*) during which we assume, as God's gift, the same gaze in judging reality and ask ourselves: what conversion of the mind, the heart and life does the Lord ask of us?

Before the prayerful reader of the word of God rises ideally the figure of Mary, the Mother of the Lord, who "treasured all these things and pondered them in her heart" (Lk 2:19; cf. 2:51), that is—as the original Greek says—finding the profound knot that unites apparently distinct events, acts and things in the great divine plan. The attitude of Mary, the sister of Martha can also be proposed to the faithful, when they read the Bible, because she sits at the feet of the Lord listening to his word, not allowing external concerns to absorb her soul completely, allowing even the free time for "the better part" which must not be taken away (cf. Luke 10:38-42).

10. Finally, we reach the last pillar that supports the Church, the house of the word: the *koinonía*, brotherly love, another name for the *agápe*, that is to say, Christian love. As Jesus mentioned, to become his brothers and his sisters one must be like "those who hear the word of God and put it into practice" (Luke 8:21). Authentic hearing is obeying and acting. It means making justice and love blossom in life. It is offering, in life and in society, a witness like the call of the prophets, which continuously united the word of God and life, faith and rectitude, worship and social commitment. This is what Jesus stated many times, beginning with the famous warning in the Sermon on the Mount: "It is not anyone who says to me, 'Lord, Lord', who will enter the kingdom of Heaven, but the person who does the will of my Father in heaven" (Matt 7:21). This phrase seems to echo the divine word proposed by Isaiah: "this people approaches me only in words, honors me only with lip-service, while their hearts are far from me" (29:13). These warnings also concern the churches when they are not faithful to the obedient hearing of the word of God.

Therefore, this must already be visible and legible on the face and in the hands of the faithful, as suggested by Saint Gregory the Great who saw in Saint Benedict, and in other great men of God, witnesses of communion with God and with their sisters and brothers, the word of God come to life. The just and faithful man not only "explains" the Scriptures, but also "unfolds" them before all as a living and practiced reality. This is why *viva lectio, vita bonorum*, the life of the good is a living lecture/lesson of the word of God. Saint John Chrysostom had already observed that the apostles came down from the mount in Galilee, where they had met the risen Lord, without any written stone tablets as Moses had: their lives would become the living gospel, from that moment on.

In the house of the word we also encounter brothers and sisters from other Churches and ecclesial communities who, even with the still existing separations, find themselves with us in the veneration and love for the word of God, the principle and source of a first and real unity, even if not a full unity. This bond must always be reinforced through the common biblical translations, the spreading of the sacred text, ecumenical biblical prayer, exegetical dialogue, the study and the comparison between the various interpretations of the Holy Scriptures, the exchange of values inherent in the various spiritual traditions and the announcement and the common witness of the word of God in a secularized world.

IV. THE ROADS OF THE WORD: MISSION

"For the Law will go forth from Zion and the word of the Lord from Jerusalem" (Is 2:3). The embodied Word of God "issues from" his house, the temple, and walks along the roads of the world to encounter the great pilgrimage that the people of earth have taken up in search of truth, justice and peace. In fact, even in the modern secularized city, in its squares and in its streets—where disbelief and indifference seem to reign, where evil seems to prevail over good, creating the impression of a victory of Babylon over Jerusalem—one can find a hidden yearning, a germinating hope, a quiver of expectation. As can be read in the book of the prophet Amos, "The days are coming, declares the Lord God, when I shall send a famine on the country: not hunger for food, not thirst for water, but famine for hearing the word of the Lord" (8:11). The evangelizing mission of the Church wants to answer this hunger.

Even the risen Christ makes an appeal to the hesitant apostles, to go forth from their protected horizon: "Go, therefore, and make disciples of all nations ... and teach them to observe the commands I gave you" (Matt 28:19-20). The Bible is fraught with appeals "not to be silent," to "speak out," to "proclaim the word at the right and at the wrong time," to be the sentinels that tear away the silence of indifference. The roads that open before us are not only the ones upon which Saint Paul and the first evangelizers traveled but are also the ones of all the missionaries who, after them, go towards the people in faraway lands.

11. Communication now casts a network that envelops the entire globe and the call of Christ gains a new meaning: "What I say to you in the dark, tell in the daylight, what you hear in whispers, proclaim from the housetops" (Matt 10:27). Of course, the sacred word must have its primary transparency and diffusion through the printed text, with translations made according to the multiplicity of languages on our planet. But the voice of the divine word must echo even through the radio, the information highway of the internet, the channels of "on line" virtual circulation, CDs, DVDs, podcasts, etc. It must appear on all television and movie screens, in the press, and in cultural and social events.

This new communication, in relationship to the traditional one, has created its own specific and expressive grammar and, therefore, makes it necessary not only to be technically prepared, but also culturally prepared for this task. In an age of images particularly provided by the dominating means of communication, such as television, the privileged model of Christ is still meaningful and evocative today. He would turn to the sign, the story, the example, the daily experience, the parable: "He told them many things in parables ... indeed, he would never speak to them except in parables" (Matt 13:3, 34). In proclaiming the kingdom of God,

Jesus never spoke over the heads of the people with a vague, abstract or ethereal language. Rather, he would conquer them by starting there where their feet were placed, in order to lead them, through daily events, to the revelation of the kingdom of heaven. Thus, the scene evoked by John becomes significant: "Some wanted to arrest him, but no one actually laid a hand on him. The guards went back to the chief priests and Pharisees who said to them, 'Why haven't you brought him?' The guards replied, 'No one has ever spoken like this man'" (7:44-46).

12. Christ proceeds along the streets of our cities and stops at the doorstep of our homes: "Look, I am standing at the door, knocking. If one of you hears me calling and opens the door, I will come in to share a meal at that person's side" (Rev 3:20). The family, enclosed between the domestic walls with its joys and sufferings, is a fundamental space where the word of God is to be allowed to enter. The Bible is full of small and great family stories, and the Psalmist depicts with liveliness the serene picture of a father sitting at the table, surrounded by his wife, like a fruitful vine, and by his children, "shoots of an olive tree" (Ps 128). In the same way, Christianity itself, from its origins, celebrated the liturgy in the daily home life, just as Israel entrusted the Passover celebration to the family (cf. Ex 12:21-27). The spreading of the word of God is passed on through the generations so that parents become "the first preachers of the faith" (LG 11). Once more the Psalmist recalled that: "What we have heard and know, what our ancestors have told us, we shall not conceal from their descendants, but will tell to a generation still to come: the praises of the Lord, his power, the wonderful deeds he has done.... They should be sure to tell their own children" (Ps 78:3-4.6).

Therefore, every home should have its own Bible and safeguard it in a visible and dignified way, to read it and to pray with it, while, at the same time, the family should propose forms and models of a prayerful, catechetical and didactic education on how to use the Scriptures, so that "young men and women, old people and children together" (Ps 148:12) may hear, understand, glorify and live the word of God. In particular, the new generations, children and youth, should be the ones receiving an appropriate and specific pedagogy that leads them to experience the fascination of the figure of Christ, opening the door of their mind and their heart, as well as through the encounter with and authentic witness of adults, the positive influence of friends and the great company of the ecclesial community.

13. Jesus, in his parable of the sower, reminds us that there are arid lands, full of rocks, choked by thorns (cf. Matt 13:3-7). He who goes forth into the streets of the world also discovers the slums where suffering and poverty, humiliation and oppression, marginalization and misery, physical and psychological ills and loneliness can be found. Often the stones on the road are bloody because of wars and violence; in the palaces of power, corruption meets injustice. The voices of the persecuted rise on behalf of faithfulness to their conscience and fidelity to their faith. One can be swept away by the crises of life, or a soul can be devoid of any meaning that would give sense and value to life itself. Like "phantoms who go their way, mere vapor their pursuits" (Ps 39:7), many feel the silence of God, his apparent absence and indifference, hanging over them: "How long, Lord, will you forget me? For ever? How long will you turn away your face from me?" (Ps 13:1). And, in the end, there arises for everyone, the mystery of death.

This immense sigh of suffering that rises from the earth to heaven is continuously represented by the Bible, which proposes an historical and incarnated faith. It is enough to think only of the pages marked by violence and oppression, of the harsh and continuous cry of Job, of the vehement pleas of the Psalms, of the subtle internal crisis that passes through the soul of Qoheleth, of the vigorous prophetic denunciations against social injustice. The sentence of the radical sin that appears in all its devastating force, from the beginning of humanity in a fundamental text of Genesis (chapter 3), is unconditional. In fact, the "mystery of iniquity" is present and acts in history, but it is revealed by the word of God that assures the victory of good over evil, in Christ.

But above all in the Scriptures, the figure of Christ, who begins his public ministry with a proclamation of hope for the last persons of the earth, dominates: "The spirit of the Lord is upon me, for he has anointed me to bring the good news to the afflicted. He has sent me to proclaim liberty to captives, sight to the blind, to let the oppressed go free, to proclaim a year of favor from the Lord" (Luke 4:18-19). He repeatedly places his hands on ill and diseased flesh. His words proclaim justice, instill courage to the disheartened and offer forgiveness to sinners. Finally, he himself approaches the lowest level, "he emptied himself" of his glory, "taking the form of a slave, becoming as human beings are; and being in every way like a human being, he was humbler yet, even to accepting death, death on a cross" (Phil 2:7-8).

In this way Christ feels the fear of death ("'Father,' he said, 'if you are willing, take this cup away from me'"), He experiences loneliness because of the abandonment and betrayal by friends, he penetrates the darkness of the cruelest physical pain through his crucifixion and even the darkness of the Father's silence ("My God, my God, why have you forsaken me?") (Mark 15:34) and reaches the last abyss of any man, that of death ("he gave a loud cry and breathed his last"). To him, the definition that Isaiah gave to the servant of the Lord truly can be applied: "the lowest of men, a man of sorrows" (53:3).

Even so, even in that extreme moment, he does not cease being the Son of God: in his solidarity of love and with the sacrifice of himself, he sows a seed of divinity in the finiteness and evil of humanity, in other words, a principle of freedom and salvation. With his offering of himself to us he pours out redemption on pain and death, assumed and lived by him, and also opens to us the dawn of resurrection. Therefore the Christian has the mission to announce this divine word of hope, by sharing with the poor and the suffering, through the witness of his faith in the kingdom of truth and life, of holiness and grace, of justice, of love and peace, through the loving closeness that neither judges nor condemns, but that sustains, illuminates, comforts and forgives, following the words of Christ: "Come to me, all you who labor and are overburdened, and I will give you rest" (Matt 11:28).

14. Along the roads of the world, the divine word generates for us Christians an equally intense encounter with the Jewish people, who are intimately bound through the common recognition and love for the Scripture of the Old Testament and because from Israel "so far as physical descent is concerned, came Christ" (Rom 9:5). Every page of the Jewish Scriptures enlightens the mystery of God and of humanity. They are treasures of reflection and morality, an outline of the long itinerary of the history of salvation to its integral fulfillment, and illustrate with vigor the incarnation of the divine word in human events. They allow us to fully understand the figure of Christ, who declared "Do not imagine that I have come to abolish the Law or the Prophets. I have come not to abolish but to fulfill them" (Matt 5:17). These are a way of dialogue with the chosen people, "who were adopted as children, the glory was theirs and the covenants; to them were given the Law and the worship of God and the promises" (Rom 9:4), and they allow us to enrich our interpretation of the Sacred Scriptures with the fruitful resources of the Hebrew exegetical tradition.

"Blessed be my people Egypt, Assyria my creation, and Israel my heritage" (Is 19:25). The Lord, then, spreads the protective mantle of his blessing all over the peoples of the earth: "he wants everyone to be saved and reach full knowledge of the truth" (1 Tim 2:4). We as Christians are also invited, along the roads of the world—without falling into a syncretism that confuses and humiliates our own spiritual identity, to enter into dialogue with respect towards men and women of the other religions, who faithfully hear and practice the directives of their sacred books, starting with Islam, which welcomes many biblical figures, symbols and themes in its tradition, and which offers the witness of sincere faith in the One, compassionate and merciful God, the Creator of all beings and Judge of humanity.

The Christian also finds common harmony with the great religious traditions of the Orient that teach us, in their holy writings, respect for life, contemplation, silence, simplicity, renunciation, as occurs in Buddhism. Or, as in Hinduism, they exalt the sense of the sacred, sacrifice, pilgrimage, fasting, and sacred symbols. Or, as in Confucianism, they teach wisdom and family and social values. Even to the traditional religions with their spiritual values expressed in the rites and oral cultures, we would like to pay our cordial attention and engage in a respectful dialogue with them. Also to those who do not believe in God but who endeavor to "do what is right, to love goodness and to walk humbly" (Mi 6:8), we must work with them for a more just and peaceful world, and offer in dialogue our genuine witness to the Word of God that can reveal to them new and higher horizons of truth and love.

15. In his *Letter to Artists* (1999), John Paul II recalled that "Sacred Scripture has thus become a sort of 'immense vocabulary' (Paul Claudel) and 'iconographic atlas' (Marc Chagall), from which both Christian culture and art have drawn" [5]. Goethe was convinced that the Gospel was the "mother tongue of Europe." The Bible, as it is commonly said, is "the great code" of universal culture: artists imaginatively dipped their paintbrush in that alphabet colored by stories, symbols, and figures which are the biblical pages. Musicians composed their harmonies around the sacred texts, especially the Psalms. For centuries authors went back to those old stories that became existential parables; poets asked themselves about the mystery of the spirit, infinity, evil, love, death and life, frequently gathering the poetical feelings that enlivened the biblical pages. Thinkers, men of learning and society itself frequently used the spiritual and ethical concepts (for example the Decalogue) of the word of God as a reference, even if merely in contrast. Even when the figure or the idea present in the Scriptures was deformed, it was recognized as being an essential and constitutive element of our civilization.

Because of this, the Bible—which teaches us also the *via pulchritudinis*, that is to say, the path of beauty to understand and reach God (as Ps 47:7 invites us: "learn the music, let it sound for God!")—is necessary not only for the believer, but for all to rediscover the authentic meanings of various cultural expressions and above all to find our historical, civil, human and spiritual identity once again. This is the origin of our greatness and through it we can present ourselves with our noble heritage to other civilizations and cultures, without any inferiority complex. The Bible should, therefore, be known and studied by all, under this extraordinary profile of beauty and human and cultural fruitfulness.

Nevertheless, the word of God—using a meaningful Pauline image—"cannot be chained up" (2 Tim 2:9) to a culture; on the contrary, it aspires to cross borders and the Apostle himself was an exceptional craftsman of inculturation of the biblical message into new cultural references. This is what the Church is called upon to perform even today through a delicate but necessary process, which received a strong impulse from the Magisterium of Pope Benedict XVI. She should make the word of God penetrate into the many cultures and express it according to their languages, their concepts, their symbols and their religious traditions. But she should always be able to maintain the genuine substance of its contents, watching over and controlling the risks of degeneration.

Therefore, the Church must make the values that the word of God offers to all cultures shine, so they may be purified and fruitful. As John Paul II said to the Bishops of Kenya during his trip to Africa in 1980, "inculturation will truly be a reflection of the Incarnation of the Word, when a culture, transformed and regenerated by the Gospel, brings forth from its own living tradition original expressions of Christian life, celebration and thought."

CONCLUSION

"Then I heard the voice I had heard from heaven speaking to me again. 'Go,' it said, 'and take that open scroll from the hand of the angel standing on sea and land.' I went to the angel and asked him to give me the small scroll, and he said, 'Take it and eat it; it will turn your stomach sour, but it will taste as sweet as honey.' So I took it out of the angel's hand, and I ate it and it tasted sweet as honey, but when I had eaten it my stomach turned sour" (Rev 10:8-11).

Brothers and sisters of the whole world, let us receive this invitation; let us approach the table of the word of God, so as to be nourished and live "not on bread alone but on every word that comes from the mouth of God" (Deut 8:3; Matt 4:4). Sacred Scripture—as affirmed by a great figure of the Christian culture—"has provided passages of consolation and of warning for all conditions" (B. Pascal, *Pensées* 532; ed. Brunschvicg).

The word of God, in fact, is "sweeter than honey that drips from the comb" (Ps 19:10), "Your word is a lamp for my feet, a light on my path" (Ps 119:105), but is also: "like fire, says the Lord, like a hammer shattering a rock" (Jer 23:29). It is like the rain that irrigates the earth, fertilizes it and makes it spring forth, and in doing this he makes the aridity of our spiritual deserts flourish (cf. Is 55:10-11). But it is also: "something alive and active: it cuts more incisively than any two-edged sword: it can seek out the place where soul is divided from spirit, or joints from marrow; it can pass judgment on secret emotions and thoughts" (Heb 4:12).

Our gaze is turned lovingly towards all those engaged in study, catechists and the other servants of the word of God to express our most intense and cordial gratitude for their precious and important ministry. We also address our persecuted brothers and sisters or those who are put to death because of the word of God and because of the witness they render to the Lord Jesus (cf. Rev 6:9): as witnesses and martyrs they tell us of "the power of the word" (Rom 1:16), origin of their faith, of their hope and of their love for God and for humanity.

Let us now remain silent, to hear the word of God with effectiveness and let us maintain this silence after hearing, so that it may continue to dwell in us, to live in us, and to speak to us. Let it resonate at the beginning of our day so that God has the first word and let it echo in us in the evening so that God has the last word.

Dear brothers and sisters, "All those who are with me send their greetings. Greetings to those who love us in the faith. Grace be with you all" (Tit 3:15).

Part Two

Pathways
of the
Word of God

Four Theological Reflections

The House of the Word: The Church

Pablo Virgilio S. David

The Twelfth Ordinary General Assembly of the Synod of Bishops in Rome held in October last year was concluded with a final message traditionally called a "*Nuntius*." That final message or *Nuntius* proposed a spiritual journey consisting of four phases. Part One was about "The Voice of the Word: *Revelation*." Part Two was about "The Face of the Word: *Jesus Christ*." Part Three discussed "The House of the Word: *The Church*" [that is my topic]. And, Part Four treated: "The Roads of the Word: *Mission*." [*Sa maghapong ito, ang kulang lang ay yung* "The Face of the Word," and I think, Bishop Chito will have to integrate it in his talk, *no*? *Ang* talk *ni* Bishop Chito *ay iyong* "The Voice of the Word: Revelation." "The Roads of the Word: Mission"—that is going to be given by Bishop Ted Bacani].

But, you know, these four topics were distributed to the four of us Synodal bishop-delegates in our recent CBCP retreat in Tagaytay. Bishop Chito was the one who took care of the "Voice of the Word"; Bishop Bastes treated the "Face of the Word"; I was assigned the third topic: "The House of the Word"; and, Bishop Broderick Pabillo was assigned the "Roads of the Word." [*E wala dito si* Bishop Bastes *at saka* Bishop Pabillo because this is strictly a Josefino affair, *ano ho*? So, *ang papalit kay* Bishop Pabillo *doon sa* "Roads of the Word" *ay si* Bishop Ted Bacani. *Tapos, dahil nawala yung* "Face of the Word," *e palagay ko naman e kaya nang i-integrate ni* Bishop Chito *sa kanyang* talk].

This paper is hardly really a lecture. It was an input meant for bishops on retreat. I therefore beg the audience's indulgence if this effort at echoing it turns into a vain reverberation of incoherent sound bites every now and then.

Let me begin with a question. The Word of God has a house, and for us Christians, it is indeed the Church. But, you know, if we are to take seriously our Judaeo-Christian roots, should we not first recognize that before God's Word found a home in the Church, it had earlier already found a home in the Jerusalem temple, and in the post-exilic Jewish synagogue? [*Lumalabas na po ang aking pagiging* Bible teacher]. So, I am going to take seriously as the first part of this lecture the temple and the synagogue institutions. And, with all due respect to the drafters of the *Nuntius,* allow me to begin with the same thought about the House of the Word, but with the temple and the synagogue as my points of departure.

The Jerusalem Temple, A House of Fire. I invite you to use your imagination a little for this. You know, when the Babylonians invaded Jerusalem, the first thing Nebuchadnezzar, the king of Babylon, really wanted to get from the temple was the fabled Ark of the Covenant which, as he probably knew well, was housed in that temple of Jerusalem. He must have imagined the Ark of the Covenant as a chest full of gold and silver, and many other treasures (the same way Indiana Jones and the raiders of the lost ark also imagined it to be). And this is all understandable, of course, considering that the Ark of the Covenant was the centerpiece of the sanctuary. And the fact that it was accessible only to the priests probably added to the sense of mystery of that Ark of the Covenant. But when Nebuchadnezzar ransacked the temple and finally seized the famous ark, I imagine his great disappointment when he found out there was nothing in the Ark of the Covenant but two stone tablets on which words were engraved, and a piece of cloth that contained something that looked like stale bread, which was supposedly the remnant of the manna, the bread God had given the Israelites in the desert (Ex 16:33). Can you imagine his disappointment? He was looking for treasures, and he found two stones. Realizing perhaps what a fool Nebuchadnezzar had made of himself, he must have hurled these stone tablets and the stale bread into the rubble, carted away the chest (because at least the chest itself was coated in gold) and demolished the temple with fury.

Nebuchadnezzar obviously did not know what those stone tablets were worth to Israel. He did not know that they had meant everything to them. They were the heart and soul of the temple because they represented the people's covenant with their God Yahweh. The words engraved on those stone tablets were God's Word to Israel. God had given his word to them—they were to be his people; he was to be their God, if they followed the commandments. This was the very foundation of their whole sense of meaning and purpose as a people. The covenant, the heart of the Torah, was their source of fire. That is why, inside the temple, before the Holy of Holies, a perpetual fire was supposed to be kept burning. The house that Nebuchadnezzar had destroyed was the house of the Word, and thus symbolically also a house of fire. The fire was meant to remind them how their God had spoken to Moses in a burning bush. God's Word was Israel's source of fire. Thus, we hear the Psalmist saying, "Your Word, O Lord, is a lamp to my feet and a light to my path" (Ps 119:105).

Perhaps we can compare Nebuchadnezzar to the thief who broke into the Adoration Chapel of a parish church in some place one night in order to steal the sacred vessels. And, the thief was obviously trying to cart away the monstrance. Afraid that he might be noticed, the thief first blew out the fire, the fire of the oil lamp, the vigil lamp. And of course, since he did not know what the Blessed Sacrament was all about, he even found time to examine the monstrance and to unhook the latch that held its glass door. He looked inside and he saw this piece of wafer. When he discovered that it was nothing but a seemingly worthless piece of bread, he left it on the altar and ran away with the golden monstrance. What a commotion there was when the sacristan discovered that they had just been burglarized. The parish priest came in really distraught, worried that the Blessed Sacrament had been desecrated. But he let out a sigh of relief when he discovered the Sacred Host lying on the altar. He turned at his panicking parishioners, smiled and said, "Oh my dear parishioners, do not you worry. The stupid thief ran away with just the container; he left the treasure." The stupid fool! He thought what we treasure in the chapel was the gold. No, no, no. It was that seemingly worthless piece of wafer. It means everything to us. And so, the parish priest took the Host, put it in a corporal, and lit again the vigil lamp.

Our Catholic tabernacle with the sacred species inside and the perpetual fire of the vigil lamp—all of these are remnants of our Judaic background. Some of you would probably remember that when I was ordained bishop at the Manila Cathedral three years ago on July 10, I shared my vocation story during my post-communion speech, and it had to do with the vigil lamp and the Jewish idea of the perpetual fire in the Jerusalem temple as a symbol of divine presence. My love affair with God really started when I was a little boy, about the age of four. Our parish catechist told us that there was a way to know if God was in the church or not. The signal is the vigil lamp; if the vigil lamp is on fire, then Jesus is there in the tabernacle. And that really, really stirred my imagination. I would visit the church regularly just to check if Jesus was there. I did not know what to say really, except to report: "Present."

The Book of Leviticus tells us the temple priests had

one important task to do, day in and day out—and that was look after the perpetual fire in the temple's sanctuary area, to keep it aflame. [*Iyon ang trabaho ng pari:* to keep the fire burning. *Kaya nga nasabi ko rin noong* ordination *ko, ang trabaho pala ng pari ay manggatong, mag-alaga ng apoy—hindi maglaro ng apoy! Pumalakpak sila* when I said that].

Leviticus 6:12-13 reads: "The fire on the altar shall be kept burning; it shall never go out. Every morning the priest shall add wood to it, lay out the burnt offering on it, and turn into smoke the fat pieces of the offerings of well-being. A perpetual fire shall be kept burning on the altar; it shall never go out." Sometimes, people think that the fire is just for the holocaust. *Hindi po totoo iyon.* The holocaust is secondary; it is the fire that is important. What is essential is the Presence, the perpetual presence of the fire.

Fire is a universal religious symbol not just for Christianity and Judaism, but for many other religions as well. We are told by anthropologists that the first temples erected by prehistoric stone-age human beings were literally "houses of fire." At a time when stone-age man did not yet know how to make fire, fire was regarded as a rare but extremely useful instrument of the gods that was bestowed upon them during occasional thunderstorms. The ancient Greeks have a mythological character called Prometheus who is supposed to have stolen fire from the gods and was punished for it.

Imagine the fascination of human beings in the primeval times over fire and its versatile uses—how it could scare animals away, how it could destroy a whole forest of trees, how it could provide light in the dark and warmth in the cold, how it could melt hard metals, etc. But since they did not know how to create fire yet, they thought it was a gift from heaven. They guarded it like a treasure in their ancient temples and their priests were guardians of the sacred fire.

They protected it from the rain and the wind, and from their enemies who might want to steal it. Since they did not yet know how to make it, their only means of retrieving it in case they lost it, was to send one of their members deep into the jungle in a serious quest for fire. They would wait for lightning to strike the forest and set some trees on fire.

The Word of God is the fire that the Jerusalem temple was built to house, the fire of divine presence that Moses had encountered, and whose Word he had engraved on stone. It was the priests' task to keep that fire burning for their people. Around the end of the seventh century, one day, Jeremiah stood at the gate of the house of the Lord and delivered his famous temple sermon denouncing corruption in the Israelite society and the total absence of compassion for the aliens, the widows, the orphans, and the poor (Jer 7:1-15). He felt that their priests were just going through the motions in the temple, that there was nothing left but empty ritualism. "The temple's fire had gone out" was the message of Jeremiah. *"Wala nang apoy ang templo!* There is no use going to this temple. *Huwag ninyong ipagmayabang ang templong ito.* The temple of the Lord … the temple of the Lord … it will be reduced to a pile of ruins!"

Many centuries later, Jesus would do the same thing in the temple they had rebuilt after the exile. He predicted the destruction of the temple for the same reason: its fire had gone out. He went in and drove away those selling and buying there, overturned the tables of the money changers and said, quoting the words of Isaiah and Jeremiah, "My house shall be called a house of prayer for all peoples. But you have made it a den of thieves" (Is 56:7; Jer 7:11).

From a House of Fire to a Pile of Ruins. In two parallel instances, a prophetic word was pronounced over the House of the Lord in Jerusalem—Jeremiah in the Old Testament and

Jesus in the New Testament. In both instances, the prophet denounced a house that had devolved into a marketplace, a den of thieves, an impressive building that had become empty and devoid of meaning because it had run out of fire—the fire of mercy and compassion. It was a structure that was ready for demolition.

Thus, we have Jesus in the Gospel reacting to the disciples' admiration for the stones and the buildings in the temple. One day, we are told, Jesus was walking with his disciples, and the disciples were admiring the beautiful stones of the temple, that have been quarried by King Herod in Jerusalem using slaves. Jesus said to them: "Do you see these great buildings? Not one stone will be left here upon another; all will be thrown down" (Mark 13:2). Having said this, he had just predicted the fall of Jerusalem to the Romans the way Jeremiah had predicted the same thing but under the Babylonians. Jesus knew why the temple had to be destroyed—it no longer housed the fire of God's Word. On another instance he would pronounce these prophetic words: "I came to bring fire to the earth, and how I wish it were already kindled" (Luke 12:49). The ambivalence of his words seemed every bit deliberate; he could have meant both the fire of God's judgment on the one hand, and the fire of God's mercy and compassion on the other hand.

In speaking this way, Jesus is following a long line of prophets ahead of him—guarding the guardians of the fire in the temple, making sure they did not douse the perpetual fire that burned inside God's house—the fire of God's Word. The prophets Amos and Isaiah did this; so did Micah and Jeremiah, as we have already noted. Jeremiah is the most classic among them because he was literally breathing fire and brimstone. The Word of the Lord came out of him in the form of scorching oracles of doom that got him into trouble. Once, he lamented about his fate and almost swore not to speak God's Word anymore. He said, "the word of the Lord has brought me reproach and derision all day long. If I say, 'I will not mention him, or speak any more in his name,' then within me there is something like a fire burning in my heart imprisoned in my bones; I grow weary holding it in, I cannot endure it" (Jer 20:8-9). Poor Jeremiah! He did not realize that the fire that no longer burned in the temple was now burning in his heart.

The Post-Exilic Synagogue, New Home of God's Word. Jerusalem was home not just to God's Word but also to God's people. And so, they felt like orphans when they lost their holy city to the Babylonians, when it was reduced to a pile of ruins and they found themselves as strangers in a foreign land. From aliens, they only began to feel at home again in foreign lands when they assembled together to listen to the Word of God, the Torah. These assemblies later became associated with the homes in which they were held— synagogues (*synagogen* = Greek: "to congregate"). But quite unlike the Jerusalem temple where the central act of worship was the offering of holocaust or animal sacrifice by the priests on behalf of the assembly, in these synagogues the main act of worship was the gathering together around the Torah, the Word of God. The Word was like the fireplace around which the community warmed itself during cold nights. The synagogue became the new house of the Word.

The synagogues of course were a far cry from the Jerusalem temple that was impressive and huge. The synagogues were little houses. Actually, they started as private homes that became centers for Bible study and for communal reflection led by their teacher, the rabbi. Compared to the glorious temple built by Solomon and later rebuilt by Herod the Great, the synagogue was a mere *barung-barong*. And yet, in these synagogues the Jews retained the symbolism of the perpetual fire in a vigil lamp next to a niche that contained the

Torah. No wonder, even as they lived in alien lands far away from their homeland, in these humble shacks they called their synagogues, their hearts burned once again with hope as they listened to their Scriptures proclaimed and interpreted to them by their rabbis. As long as they had God's Word, even if they had lost their land, their king, their temple, and their holy city, they somehow felt at home again. Home, they realized, did not have to be their temple. Home did not mean a return to their actual homeland. Home was wherever they continued to gather around the Torah, as a people of the covenant, witnessing to the Gentiles and even welcoming them in their company. They started to open the Word of God to non-Jews. Unlike the Jerusalem temple which was exclusive to the Jews, the synagogue was for everyone. The house was for all people, for all nations.

We have an old saying in *Kapampangan* that says:

"Map ne kaku bale-dampa nung karin bie ku timawa.
Kesa ketang bale tisa a nun nu ku makasila't
*   sasakmalan ning upaya."*
[Better for me a humble shack where my life is free than a house made of tiles but where I am in shackles and a slave of masters].

It is our own version of the more popular Tagalog saying that goes:

"Mabuti na sa akin ang bahay kahit kubo kung nakatira ay tao
Kaysa bahay na bato na ang nakatira naman ay kuwago."
[Better for me a lowly hut that is home to human beings than a proud stone castle that has only owls for its dwellers].

Filipinos are keenly aware of the difference between a house and a home (*bahay at tahanan*). It is one thing to build a

house and another to make a home. Alas, not every house is
a home. The temple saw its end, the moment it stopped being
a home to the Word of God. In the 1970s, there was a popular
song that expressed this thought romantically.

"A chair is still a chair even when there's no one
    sitting there.
But a chair is not a house, and a house is not a home
when there's no one there to hold you tight
and no one there you can kiss good night."

"A room is still a room, even when there's nothing
    there but gloom.
But a room is not a house, and a house is not a home
when the two of us are far apart
and one of us has a broken heart."

How romantic, *pero totoo naman*. Just putting together
two people under one roof does not mean you have a family
already. Sometimes people live under one roof and yet they
have broken hearts and they are not on speaking terms.
Sometimes, they even share the same bed, and yet they
despise each other. How can there be a home there?

The homely synagogues that housed the Word of
God soon also became exclusive institutions all over again.
Not only did they make the Gentiles feel unwelcome, they
made no space even for the prophet who made God's voice
resound there and disturb them as Jesus did in the synagogue
in Nazareth. Mark tells us "they took offense at him," and
that their lack of faith prevented him from performing mighty
deeds there (Mark 6:1-6). In Luke 4:28-29, after Jesus read from
the prophet Isaiah, and after he commented on it [which must
have been the shortest homily ever for all he said was "Today,
this scripture passage is fulfilled in your hearing"], they took
offense at him. They even went to the extent of attempting to

kill him. Luke 4 says that "they were filled with rage. They got up and drove him out and led him to the brow of the hill so that they might hurl off that cliff." Why? Because he had pronounced the prophetic word. The fire of the prophet was not welcome in the synagogue anymore.

The rejection of Jesus in the synagogue of Nazareth was a foretaste of the later expulsion of the Christians from the synagogues. The Christians were not welcome anymore in the Houses of the Word of God, because they claimed to have found the Word of God in a fellow human being called Jesus of Nazareth. They claimed to have found in Jesus the Face of the Word. The new venues for their gatherings would now be—among others—a lakeshore, a hillside, a boat, a road, a private home—wherever "two or three" could gather in Jesus' name. The Word of God had just built a new home in the *ekklesia.*

The Church, an Open House for the Word and for the World. The early Christians gathered together in their homes in order to partake of God's Word and the Eucharist. These early house churches (*ekklesie kat'oikon*) were really private homes that were gradually restructured to accommodate the *ekklesia* (assembly) of several households. To give a rough description of the gradual transformation of the typical Greco-Roman *domus* into a house-church, I recommend that we take a look at Paul's strongly worded critique of the table fellowships of the Corinthian community. In First Corinthians 11, Paul does not mince word in scolding the Corinthians for their scandalous behavior during their Eucharistic gatherings at which some members supposedly indulged in lavish food and wine, while others went hungry. This was perfectly understandable in the context of the class division right within a typical Roman household, as evidenced by the architecture of the typical *domus* (house). Even as they gathered in the home setting as a "community of disciples" they continued to be bound by the Roman culture which dictated where particular members of the household were supposed to position themselves: the spaces for the women and children were distinguished from the spaces for the men; the Gentiles from the Jews, and the slaves from the freemen.

The front part of a typical *domus* was reserved for the masters—the *atrium* (open hall), the *cubicula* (masters' bedrooms), the *triclinium* (the dining room), the *culina* (the kitchen) and the *tablinum* (office), while the back part was the space for the servants, the slaves and the workmen: the *peristylium* (colonnaded garden) with its own cubicles, kitchen and dining area, and an enclosed garden called *exedra* [which, I presume, is a euphemism for toilet]. Perhaps Paul's reaction seemed even strange to the community because as Roman citizens, these Corinthians had known no other lifestyle than this system of segregation. Actually, Paul even seemed ready to tolerate this customary segregation, as long as it did not involve their Eucharists. "Do you not have houses in which you can eat and drink?" (1 Cor 11:22). For him, the Eucharist went against the very grain of the Roman culture of class segregation. For him, the Eucharist must unite the community as brothers and sisters. Thus, he insisted elsewhere that in the community of Christ, "There is no longer Jew or Greek, there is no longer slave or free, there is no longer male and female; for all of you are one in Christ Jesus" (Gal 3:28). In short, a house that serves as a home to the Word and the Eucharist has to allow itself to be restructured and transformed by the Word. Because they receive the one body of Christ, they are to grow into the body of Christ. When Paul admonishes the Corinthians to "wait for each other" at their table fellowships, the radical implication of this admonition is that the community must learn to let go of what we in modern parlance might call a cultural *apartheid*. In the community of Christ, the freemen must now learn to eat with their slaves and workers, whom they now were obliged by the Gospel to treat as family. Recall how Paul wrote an endorsement letter to Philemon on account of his runaway slave Onesimus—asking Philemon to accept Onesimus, no longer as a slave but as a brother.

Thus, even architecturally, it is understandable why the dividing wall of the *tablinum* that separated the masters' quarters from that of the servants was eventually demolished, transforming the whole *atrium* and the *peristylium* into one common hall which eventually became the nave of the church, and pushing the *tablinum* to the further end so that it became the area for the altar and the *cathedra*. It had to make way for the Word. The Community that lives in Christ has only Christ and no other as its head. Every part is a member of the same body—Christ's. Transformed by the Word and nourished by the Word-made-flesh, the Church becomes a fitting home of the Word. Thus Paul has every reason to assure the Ephesians that they were "no longer strangers and aliens, but you are citizens with the saints and also members of the household of God, built upon the foundation of the apostles and prophets, with Christ Jesus himself as the cornerstone. In him the whole structure is joined together and grows into a holy temple in the Lord; in whom you also are built together spiritually into a dwelling place for God" (Eph 2:19-22).

From architecture we can shift to the analogy of agriculture, but the idea remains the same: the Word of God needs a home. Like the seed for the sowing, the Word does not germinate in a soil that is barren, hard, rocky, or full of thorns. God's Word can germinate only in the good soil. Remember Mark 4:1-20. I remember when I was a seminarian, I spent sometime in Cabiao, Nueva Ecija for my apostolate with the farmers. One day we were having a Bible study and we were reflecting on Mark 4, the parable of the sower. One of the farmers shared some reflection: *"Ay mahinang klase ho yung magsasaka na yan, di marunong." "Sino?" sabi ko. "Yung magsasaka diyan sa Ebanghelyo," sabi niya. "Ay kung mahusay siyang magsasaka, bakit kung saan-saan nahuhulog ang binhi niya? May nahulog sa daanan. May nahulog sa mabato. May mga nahulog sa mga dawag, sa mga damu-damo."* "He's not a good farmer," he said. "He is throwing his seeds everywhere. Any good farmer would know that the main task is not really the sowing. The sowing comes last. The more important task of the farmer is soil preparation, making the earth a fitting home to the seed—irrigate it, weed it, cultivate it." God's word is like the seed. It can only be at home on the good soil of humility, the loose soil that has been plowed by trials and tests, the fertile soil that has known death and decay. Only this kind of soil can become a home to the seed so that it bears much fruit (John 12:24).

The opposite of "at-homeness" is alienation. [*Sa Tagalog, ang* opposite *ay "namamahay." Kapag namamahay ka, di ka makatulog*]. It is the state of estrangement best described by the Jewish experience of exile, which in turn is beautifully allegorized in Genesis by the banishment of Adam and Eve from the Garden of Eden (Gen 3). The human quest for God becomes a quest for home—pictured in the Book of Revelation as God's dwelling place (Revelation 21:3): "And I heard a loud voice from the throne saying, 'See, the home of God is among mortals. He will dwell with them; they will be his people, and God himself will be with them'." This divine home among mortals is pictured as an altogether new temple, a "new Jerusalem"—namely, no longer a mere structure but a relationship, a renewed covenant. If we are to suppose that the same writer is behind the Fourth Gospel, then indeed we can describe this "new home" as a home of the Word, "If anyone loves me, he will keep my word, and my Father will love him and we will come to him and make our home with him" (John 14:23). To "keep the Word" is to live in the covenant-*agape* of Father and Son.

Four Pillars of the House of the Word. Borrowing from the Old Testament description of divine wisdom building a house among mortals and supporting it with seven pillars (Prov. 9:1), the Synod *Nuntius* presents the Church as home of the Word, built on the four pillars of (1) the teaching of the apostles (*didache*), (2) the fellowship (*koinonia*), (3) the breaking of the bread (*klasei tou artou*), and (4) the prayers (*tais proseuchais*). "They devoted themselves to the apostles' *teaching* and *fellowship*, to the *breaking of bread* and the *prayers*" (Acts 2:42).

FIRST PILLAR: THE *DIDACHE* (THE TEACHING OF THE APOSTLES. The *Nuntius* highlights preaching, catechesis, and the homily, as the major occasions in the Church for the handing down of the Gospel of Christ through the teaching of the apostles. They "presuppose a reading and understanding, an explaining and interpreting, and involvement of the mind and heart" (*Nuntius* 7). They aim to achieve the dual movement of exegesis and theology—of the Word as it was originally proclaimed and meant in its own historical context, and of the same Word as it is understood and lived by its present-day hearers and readers. The first "goes back to the roots of the sacred texts, the events, the first words of the history of salvation, in their meaning and in their message." The second aims to "return to the present, to the today lived by those who hear and read." This dual movement is what we see in the conversation between Jesus and the disciples at Emmaus (Luke 24:13-35), as well as in the dialogue between Philip and the Ethiopian official in Acts 8:30-31. The finality remains one and the same—a full encounter with Christ, the Word Incarnate.

SECOND PILLAR: THE BREAKING OF THE BREAD (THE EUCHARIST). To the two disciples on the road to Emmaus, the preaching that Jesus did on the Law and the Prophets was just preparatory for a fuller encounter—in the breaking of the bread, which facilitates and effects the act of recognition: "their eyes were opened" (Luke 24:31). Luke rightly regards the Eucharist as the new covenant sealed in the blood of Christ (Luke 22:20), the "supreme work of the Word who offers himself as food in his immolated body ... the source and summit of the life and mission of the Church" (*Nuntius* 8). It is called a "memorial," not just in the sense of recalling a past event, but in the most Jewish sense of remembering—which means a "making present," a re-actualization of the paschal event, at which the faithful receive, through the Church, "the Bread of Life from the table both of God's Word and Christ's Body" (DV 21). Word and Eucharist are supposed to "... form but one single act of worship" (SC 56).

THIRD PILLAR: THE PRAYERS. The house of the Word has "the prayers" as one of its pillars. Note that it goes with the definitive article "the," which suggests that we are not referring here to prayers in the generic sense—or whenever one might feel like praying. "The prayers," in the tradition of the Church are regular prayer periods that Christianity has inherited from Judaism, consisting of "psalms, hymns, and inspired songs," as mentioned by Paul in Col. 3:16.

They are best represented by the Liturgy of the Hours, which, unfortunately, have been associated mainly with the discipline of the ordained and those in the religious life. "The Prayers" are a traditional component of all the so-called religions of the Book—Judaism, Christianity and Islam. Of the three, it would seem that Islam has remained more consistent about insisting on the observance of "the prayers" at particular times of the day, not just among its clerics, but among their faithful in general. You think that is original to Islam? No, it is original to Judaism. During the exilic period, the Jews were told to pray facing Jerusalem six times a day. In Daniel 6:10, Daniel gets into trouble because his detractors have caught him in the act of performing his regular prayers while facing the direction of Jerusalem.

That is why we Christians have Morning prayer, Midmorning prayer, Midday prayer, Midafternoon prayer, Evening prayer, and Night prayer. And, this is not only for the religious and the ordained. This is for all Christians. The Liturgy of the Hours must not be a monopoly of the religious. It is a part of our tradition that several times a day, Christians pause for a while to pray using hymns, psalms, and inspired songs.

That is why the poor and illiterate before would go to the monasteries to beg them to let them participate in the prayers. But the monks used books called breviaries; and because they could not produce enough books for everybody, they invented the Rosary, the "prayer of the poor and the illiterate," the "breviary of the uneducated." They created the bead prayer (which came from the Oriental tradition), because the poor could not afford the breviary which contained the psalms. Indeed, the Rosary is such a beautiful tradition of the Church. It is contemplative and biblical. It asks us to meditate on the mysteries of our faith: the infancy, life, death, and resurrection of our Lord. That is why we have the Joyful, Sorrowful, and Glorious Mysteries, and lately, Pope John Paul II added the Luminous mysteries.

The *Nuntius* likewise mentions the inclusion of *lectio divina*, i.e., a prayerful reading of the Scriptures, and its contribution to the enrichment of "the prayers of the Church." As far as I can recall, there was probably not a single day during the duration of the Synod that the *lectio divina* was not mentioned. Different approaches were shared by bishops from different countries especially of Latin America and Africa. But the general pattern remains the same:

- *Lectio:* We read the text and ask: "What is the Biblical text saying in itself?"
- *Meditatio:* We reflect on it and ask: "What is the text saying to us?"
- *Oratio:* We ask, "What do we say to the Lord in answer to His Word?"
- *Contemplatio:* We ask, "What conversion of the mind, heart, and life is the Lord asking of us?"

The *Nuntius* likewise proposes the two Marys (the Mother of Jesus and the sister of Martha and Lazarus) as Biblical models *par excellence* for prayer (Luke 2:19, 52 and Luke 10:38-42).

FOURTH PILLAR: *KOINONIA* (FELLOWSHIP). *Koinonia* is the pillar that Paul felt was missing from the Corinthian community despite their ritual meals. He dared say that what they were partaking was "not the Lord's Supper," because it was not effecting the *agape* of Christ that this meal stood for (1 Cor 11:20-21): "When you come together, it is not really to eat the Lord's Supper. For when the time comes to eat, each of you goes ahead with your own supper, and one goes hungry and another becomes drunk."

For Paul, there can be no Eucharist in a community whose members do not love one another. Without love, there can be no Eucharist. Thus, Paul warned them sternly in 1 Corinthians 11:27-29: "Whoever, therefore, eats the bread or drinks the cup of the Lord in an unworthy manner will be answerable for the body and blood of the Lord." In other words, there can be no communion with Christ in a gathering where the members despise one other or have no communion with one another. They are ranked, not among those who are nourished and saved by the body and blood of Christ, but rather among those who murdered Christ. The body of

Christ whom they receive will effect not their salvation but rather their condemnation.

In Pampanga, the late Bishop Cesar Ma. Guerrero, our first bishop, followed this same Pauline discourse when he addressed the violence and the killings resulting from the agrarian conflict in the province in the 1950s. When he took over its local Church, Pampanga was the killing fields of the Philippines. Back then, both the peasants and the *haciendeross* (who were all Catholics) were arming themselves to the teeth, ambushing and murdering each other, even as they attended the same Eucharist on Sundays in their parish churches and barrio chapels. The late Bishop Guerrero observed this and denounced it publicly. One day, he celebrated Mass in San Fernando and delivered a strongly worded homily in one of his Masses, as he promoted what he called a *"Cruzada de Caridad y Penitencia"* of the *Virgen de los Remedios,* patroness of Pampanga, and *Santo Cristo del Perdon.* He delivered a prophetic speech that hurt the sensitivities of the *Kapampangans.* He said, *"Aqui en Pampanga, hay mucha piedad pero poca caridad"* [Here in Pampanga, there is much piety but so little charity]. *Aray!* It sounded "Jeremiah-nic." But the people could not walk out because the *Virgen* and the *Santo Cristo* were there. They could only respond with filial piety. Bishop Guerrero had just dismissed as nothing but pure pietism the attendance of both parties in common Eucharistic gatherings that had no effect whatsoever on their behavior and their regard for one another. He challenged them to prove their faith in action— through dialogue for peace, through Christian charity to the poor, the best expression of which was not just the sharing of food, but also the sharing of land. He said: "What will you do with thousands of hectares of land while the poor are languishing?" It was very difficult for the *hacienderos* to take. But that was the beginning of land reform in the Philippines. It started in my province, in Pampanga. And, what ended it was our *Cruzada de Caridad y Penitencia.*

The *Nuntius* characterizes *koinonia* (fraternal love), as "another name for *agape*, that is to say, Christian love" (*Nuntius* 10). It is not to be confused with just any kind of fellowship. It is fellowship with Christ, and in Christ. To become brother, sister, or mother to Christ, is to "hear the Word of God and put it into practice" (Luke 8:21). To hear the Word and put it into practice in *koinonia,* in fellowship, is what gives solidity to the house of the Word. Thus Jesus says, "Everyone then who hears these words of mine and acts on them will be like a wise man who built his house on rock.... And, everyone who hears these words of mine and does not act on them will be like a foolish man who built his house on sand" (Matt 7:24, 26).

Conclusion. The Church, the new house that God has built in Jesus Christ, is meant to be a home, not just to the Word but to the whole world. It is imbued with the openness and welcoming spirit that its builder has designed it with, where even sinners and tax-collectors, prostitutes and lepers, Gentiles and slaves, and all others who are excluded can now find a home. That is what it means to be Catholic. Catholic means to be inclusive, to be open to everyone, specially the last, the least, and the lost. Thus, Jesus says, "In my Father's house there are many dwelling places" (John 14:2). In the new house we call the Church, there are many rooms. There is a lot of open space—members must learn to keep an open mind and an open heart towards one another.

The Voice of the Word: Revelation

Luis Antonio G. Tagle

We would like to thank the Academic Committee of San Jose Seminary for organizing this forum. In fact, the first invitation for me was to address the seminarians about my doctoral dissertation—how I chose the topic, etc. It has become now a massive operation open to the public. It has become more formal, as seen in the apparel. And just like Cardinal Rosales, when you are back to San Jose, you are a child once again and you have to obey. You obey even the seminarians.

It has been customary that at the end of a Synod, the Fathers would issue a message to the People of God. It is not a summary of the Synod, but it is a way of sharing some of the orientations and basic insights that came from the deliberations of the bishops for three weeks. And since the Synod is devoted to the theme "The Word of God in the Life and Mission of the Church," the Message focused on different dimensions of the Word of God.

The Message used the following images: the Voice of the Word, the Face of the Word, the House of the Word and the Paths of the Word. My task is to provide some reflections on Revelation based on the image of the Voice of the Word used in the Message. I will follow the points found in the Message [*Nuntius*]. There are four main points regarding the Voice of the Word.

Understanding Revelation as the Voice of the Word.
Someone asked me, "How come God is Trinity? *Bakit may tatlong persona, subalit iisa ang Diyos? Sinong nag-imbento niyan? Mas madaling maniwala sa isang Diyos. Yung isa na naging tatlo, at tatlo na naging isa, napakahirap. Sinong nag-imbento niyan? Ihahabla ko!*" I said, "Nobody invented it. That was how God revealed God-self." Our faith rests on revelation. We do not fabricate it. We just receive in obedience what God has revealed to us.

The Message utilizes the metaphor of *Voice* to present Revelation. It refers to Deuteronomy 4:12 where Moses tells the people, "Then the Lord spoke to you from the midst of the fire. You heard the sound of the words, but saw no form. There was only a voice." God comes not through a visible form but through a voice, a voice that conveys words. The voice of God is the bearer of God's word. There are those people who are so used to trying to detect the presence of God through sight; this is not bad. But in the Old Testament, Moses tells us, many times it is through a voice.

I would like to make some observations on Revelation as *Voice*. First of all, God is presented as the God who speaks, who communicates, and who dialogues. Metaphorically we are told that the word of God is communicated through His voice. The word has a voice. The word needs a voice. A voice carries the word to its destined hearer. As far as the Bible is concerned, the voice of God is not merely a sound but an event of the word.

This observation can be made of the human voice as well. Jeremiah tells God that in his prayer, "that which came out of my lips was before Thy face" (Jer 17:16). What is that which comes before the face of God in the prayerful voice of Jeremiah? We can also ask what is that which comes before our face when the voice of God reaches us. *Kapag ako nagsalita*

*at may tinig ako, ano iyong dumarating sa harapan ninyo? Tunog
lang ba?* Whether it is the voice of God or of a human being,
it seems that a voice gives exterior form and presence to what
the interiority of the heart wants to say. The voice expresses
the word that is not merely in the heart, but the word that *is*
the heart. The heart is the word.

The voice of God (or that of a human being) reveals
the heart or soul (*loob / kalooban*) of God (or of the human
person). In the holistic approach of the Bible, the heart that
is externalized in the voice includes the thoughts, sentiments,
intentions, plans, designs and decisions of a person, in this
case, of the personal God. *Sa tinig ng Diyos, nakikita natin ang
kanyang puso. At nasa puso ng Diyos ang kanyang mga naiisip at
nararamdaman, mga panukala, mga plano. Iyan ang puso, iyan ang
salita.* The voice "names" the mysterious "within" by giving
expression to the "content" of the heart. The voice indeed is
a vehicle of the revealing of the identity of the one speaking.
When one speaks, the word that arises is one's heart. So is it
with God's voice.

I have to make a confession. *Kahit isang taon na po yung*
"The Word Exposed" [Sunday Bible Reflection Program], *sa
tuwing shoot* [filming], *kinakabahan ako*, not because I come
unprepared. I usually come over-prepared. I have so many
things there that I do not need to say during the shoot. But
what really makes me afraid is this. After exposing, after
giving voice to what I thought was contained in the Word, I
know I have revealed my heart. And I feel so exposed. I am
afraid; what am I making public? You know I am a private
person. I am basically shy. Father Vic, *maniwala ka?* Really.
My relatives often tell me, "*Ikaw pa naman iyong taong ayaw
humarap sa tao noong bata ka. Ngayon, ikaw ang laging pinahaharap
sa napakaraming tao.*" I really suffer. This is not my cup of tea.
Really, after giving voice to something, I feel somehow, it is
not just the words. It is the word that is the heart; it is the

person exposed for the world to see. And I tell you, I get a lot of hate-mail; yes, from those who are not Catholics, those who do not believe in what I say. Sometimes you just want to keep quiet and stop being the voice. It is not just praises that you get. You also get a lot of opposition.

So it is not just sounds, the voice conveys the word, that is the heart. The simple image of the Voice of the Word captures aptly and beautifully the event of Revelation. Through the "speaking voice" of God, the heart of God is spoken. The voice "lays bare" who God is, His thoughts, intentions, plans and decisions. This is what the theologians call the content or the *noetic* aspect of Revelation. In *Dei Verbum*, we are told that what is revealed is who God is and His saving design out of love for humanity and creation (DV 2).

To complete the picture, we come to a second observation. When a voice and its word reach their intended receiver, a new situation is effected in the heart or interiority of the listener. Husbands, *sabihin ninyo sa asawa ninyo*, "*Parang ang taba-taba mo at parang tumatanda ka.*" That will create a new situation beginning in the heart of your wife. Wives, tell your husbands, "*Alam mo yung pinakasalan ko guwapo at mabait. Ngayon, mas guwapo na yung driver natin.*" Ah, that will create a new situation in the heart of your husband. It might create a situation of insecurity, and he might want to prove that he is still dashing. *Maghahanap tuloy iyan ng iba.*

Heart affects heart. Here lies the power of the voice even in ordinary human interaction. The inflection of the voice, conveying the content of the heart of the speaker, creates something in the heart of the listener. The content of the texture of our voice can hurt or console, edify or destroy our listener. A person who gives voice to the goodness of his or her heart can generate a wholesome disposition in the heart of another person.

In biblical and dogmatic theology, it is said that the Word of God is effective and dynamic. Even sacramental theology states that a sacrament (a visible word) effects what it signifies. The voice-word event is *performative* and not merely informative. The word of God is active. It does something. Revelation is a communicative event initiated by God who makes His face and design of salvation heard; and, in the very "voicing," the saving event begins and the listener is prompted to decide and to act. That is why Jesus can say, "Today, this Scripture passage is fulfilled" (Luke 4:28-29). The Word did not merely give them information, it wants to fulfill what it contains.

That is why I usually end my reflection in "The Word Exposed" by saying, "The Word has been exposed, let us now fulfill it." Sometimes people approach me and say, "Bishop, *ang ganda ng reflection mo.*" I say, "*Salamat.* Now, do it! Let the Word do something to you." *May isa pang sumulat sa akin,* "Bishop, *anong sabon po ang ginagamit ninyo? Ang linaw-linaw ng kutis ninyo.*" *Naku po, ano ba naman iyan! Wala po akong* sponsor *sa sabon.* We exposed the Word, or maybe even, the Word is exposing itself, so that the Word will fulfill something in us.

The Voice wills to effect what it contains. But the listener will have to decide from his or her heart. The crucial question is whether the Voice of God will fall on attentive hearts or will it be wasted on stony ones. For the communicative event to be complete, the listener's heart must allow the voice to fully achieve what it intends. To fail to do so frustrates the saving event from happening in our lives.

Regarding this first point of my reflection, I invite you—and in a special way, the priests and seminarians—to examine how deeply we listen to the voice of God and allow its transforming power to take hold of us. Let me share with you something about our role as bishops. We bishops are pulled here and there. Whenever we are invited to a function, we are not left in a corner to be silent. Whenever we are invited, we are expected to say something. Our voices are heard from simple kindergarten graduation rites to the most sublime of activities. But, I want to ask us bishops, and you: "Do we, who always talk, talk, and talk, devote quality time to listening to the Voice-Word of God so that we could be renewed? Do we give quality time to listening or do we devote *mga* 'spare time' *na lang*?" Church history attests that only those who receive the "creative" Word could in turn echo the Voice of God to others. So we ask ourselves: how can we maintain and sustain a profound listening to the voice of God that often comes to us not through thunder or earthquakes but through a silent whisper? *Kapag may Ondoy at Pepeng, lahat nakikinig. Kapag walang Onoy at Pepeng at ang Diyos bumubulong na lang, may nakikinig pa kaya?* How often do we listen? Twenty times a year, corresponding to the number of typhoons? How ridiculous! *Kapag may bagyo, ang daming nagte-text:* "What is the Lord telling us? What is the Lord telling us?" *Bakit hindi sila nagte-text kapag tahimik?* There is something wrong in our listening. Do we need more Onoys and Pepengs to learn how to listen?

Revelation and the Shaping of History. We have seen how the image of the voice of God depicts the revelation of God's identity and saving plan. We also considered how God's revelatory word is active and effective. The Message of the Synod points to an important "action" of the Word of God, namely, that of originating human history.

The Message [*Nuntius*] reminds us that God speaks His voice within time and history. Some even say that God communicates through time and history. From a faith perspective, we can even say that history owes its existence to God whose voice is at the origin of human history. Through the revelation of God, human history becomes salvation history. The Bible attests to how serious God is with human history. In other words, there is an intimate connection between God's revelation and the making of history.

Using the eyes of faith, we are able to discern the dynamic presence of divine action, intervention or communication in our personal and communal histories. The peak of God's saving intervention is in Jesus Christ, the Word of God who became flesh, and by so doing, was immersed in the drama of human history. The events that make salvation history follow each other and even prepare succeeding events toward the fulfillment of the Reign of God in Jesus Christ. So the story of humanity includes what the voice of God is doing in and with human history. Revelation is not a mere communication of the content of God's identity and plan but effects in history what God intends.

We may ask the question whether all events in history are to be considered divine revelation. From the orientations provided by *Dei Verbum* of Vatican II, we hold that not all events in history qualify as Revelation in the strict sense of the term. We come to discover the revelatory character of an event through the initiative of God, whose voice interprets an event, making it speak the divine truth that it contains. Without the voice that speaks the interior word, the event is simply an occurrence. The prophets of the Bible provide a good example of how the voice-word component clarifies that a Revelation of God was unfolding in a human event.

The prophets often introduce their pronouncements with the words, "thus says the Lord" (cf. Jer 18:13-15). In the account of his calling (Jer 1:4-10), the Lord tells Jeremiah to speak whatever God commands. Then God puts out his hand and touches Jeremiah's mouth, saying, "Behold I have put my words in your mouth" (v. 9). The prophet speaks only what God tells him to utter. The prophet interprets an event not from his own perspective but from that of the Word of God placed in his mouth. The prophet becomes an important figure in showing how an event comes from God whose word gives inner meaning to an event as a divine action. But it is God who transforms a timid person like Jeremiah into a prophet. It is God's hand that makes the prophet's mouth the medium of a revelatory message and a call for the people's fidelity to their covenant with God.

At this point I would invite you to consider how much the Word of God shapes our history. We may even ask if our people find the meaning of their experiences in the light of the Word of God. You know it makes me shudder to think that maybe the soap operas or other "in" things are generating much more history in people's lives than the Word of God. *Noong minsan nga po, bumaba ako para magkape doon sa aming seminaryo. At yung mga kusinera, seryosong nag-uusap. Sabi nung isa, "Naku yang Fernando na yan, kapag di siya nag-ingat, lagot siya talaga." Sabi naman nung isa, "Aba, problema niya na yan; tigas ng ulo niya e." E dahil sila'y magkakamag-anak, akala ko ang pinag-uusapan ay isang kamag-anak na may problema. E di lumapit ako dala yung kape. Naka-upo ako doon. Habang seryoso silang pinag-uusapan yung problema ni Fernando, sinabi ko, "E ano bang maitutulong natin kay Fernando?" Tinignan nila ako at nagtawanan, "Ay* Father, *pinag-uusapan namin yung telenovela, si Fernando Jose."* This Fernando Jose was generating a new history in the lives of the cooks. I do not know if the Word of God is infusing meaning into their lives' histories.

And worse, that same year, I went to Cebu to address a congress. I was billeted in one hotel. As I was checking out, with my back turned to the front door, *biglang nagkagulo.* And all the people attending to me at the front desk left me. *Bakit kaya? Dumating pala si Fernando Jose! Nagtakbuhan sila! Yumakap sila't humalik kahit hindi nila kilala! Sabi ko, "Nandito naman ako." Iniwanan ako! E kung siya ay Fernando Jose, ako naman ay Luis Antonio; dalawa rin ang pangalan ko. Siya dala-dala niya telenovela, dala-dala ko salita ng Diyos.* But I will not make history. And, Fernando Jose probably will.

But, so many people are telling me that the hearts of the priests are revealed to them because most of their examples in their homilies come from *telenovelas*. So they say, *"Mukhang wala nang ginagawa ang mga pari kundi manood ng telenovela." At mukhang hindi lang mga pari. Sisters, mukhang kayo rin, inaagahan ang* evening prayer. *O, tuwang-tuwa kayong mga layko, e kayo rin naman.* Sometimes, you do not eat together in the dining room because you are following one episode, and you bring your plate in front of the TV. These *telenovelas* are really generating history.

If there is some truth to this, we need to discover the reason. Is it happening by default? Where have the prophets disappeared to? Where are the Jeremiahs, the Isaiahs, the Ezekiels? Where are they to be found? And, we who share in the prophetic mission of Jesus need to ask what criteria we use to interpret events whether in the lives of individuals or of society. Does the Word of God play a central role in our search for hope in our tumultuous history? Do we rely solely on human wisdoms that may contain much good and truth to the neglect of the voice of God that calls us to the wisdom guiding history? I ask these questions because people come to us pastors and preachers of the Word with the expectation of being guided in discovering the meaning of life in the light of faith. They bring their frustrations, needs, sins, wounds and dying to us so that the power of the Paschal Mystery of Jesus Christ may kindle hope and strength for the journey. What voice do they hear from us—that of an ideologue or a politician or a bitter person or a prophet who says, "thus says the Lord"?

I had confirmations in one parish. And at the of the confirmation, as we were going out of the Church, one boy asked me, "Bishop, *kayo po ba yung lumalabas sa TV, yung napapanood ko?" "Oo, ako,"* sagot ko. *Tapos, iyong bata sa likuran niya sabi, "Uy! Ang nagkumpil sa atin artista!" Naku, ayan na. Hindi na ako pari, hindi na obispo, artista na. Kapag lumabas ka sa TV, artista ka na. Naisip ko, "Bakit sila nagpakumpil sa akin? Dahil ba sa biyaya, o dahil artista ako?" E di ko naman mapigilang maging artista.*

We hope that in our voice they may hear the word that the Lord has put in every prophet's mouth. Then somehow the joyful and painful experiences begin to speak of a God who faithfully walks with them.

Creation and the Voice of the Word. The Message of the Synod of Bishops considers our faith in God the Creator and Revelation. Creation is depicted as a voice that speaks of the presence of the benevolent Creator.

Some of you might ask why we did not deal first with creation before reflecting on history. After all, creation is the first act of God towards the world. But if we look at the unfolding of Revelation in the history of the biblical people, we realize that their primordial experience of God and Revelation was the Exodus and the forging of the Covenant. God made Himself known to the future people Israel as the One who sees their sufferings, hears their cries, and desires their freedom from slavery towards worship of God. A faith conviction developed that this personal God truly created them as His people. It was God who made a non-people to become a people, and not just any form of people but the People of God based on the Covenant. This people saw how God used the powerful forces of nature to fulfill His saving plan. God exercised sovereign power over these mysterious forces. And through the long history of Israel's journey, marred by forgetfulness and infidelities, the exile was significant in crystallizing their faith. Their sins have made them a non-people again, but through the prophets the God of covenant love promised that He would restore or recreate them.

In their contact with Mesopotamian creation myths it became clearer to them that the God of exodus and covenant held everything in His powerful hands, because everything came from Him. Unlike the gods of Mesopotamia that had to subdue each other in a struggle that brought forth the universe, God created everything by His voice and word. The various creatures are not gods. They are creatures that owe their origin from a God who has a loving plan already revealed in the history of the exodus and the covenant. In biblical faith, creation is even considered the first voice of salvation that initiated the history of salvation. The world exists from the power of God's Word, the power of love that is the very heart of God. God does not have to struggle with natural forces to produce the world. God speaks His heart and the world begins to be. "By the Lord's word the heavens were made. By the breath of His mouth all their hosts. For He spoke and it came to be. He commanded and it took place" (Ps 33:3-6).

In the New Testament, Paul speaks of God who gives life to the dead and calls into existence the things that do not exist (Rom 4:17). We can already intimate the link between faith in creation and salvation in the Paschal Mystery of the Last Adam Jesus Christ (Rom 6). If God truly created everything by the power of His Word, why can God not raise the dead to life, an act of new creation through His Word made flesh?

God spoke and all came to be. Now it is the turn of creation to speak of God. "The heavens declare the glory of God. They sky proclaims its builder's craft…. There is no speech or sound; no voice is heard, yet their span goes out to all the earth and their words to the ends of the earth" (Ps 19:2-5). Creation proclaims the providence of God, not through the usual form of vocal speech, but its word nevertheless reaches to the ends of the world.

Let us not forget, however, that human beings are the apex of creation. And so, as we marvel at the beauty of the skies, the hills, the rivers, I hope that the beauty of the human person is also a voice to us of the presence of God. The sad thing is, we are captivated by the beauty of nature but we abhor human beings. *Mabuti pa ang mga tuta niyayakap, ang kanilang mga* maid *hindi mayakap. Mabuti pa ang* flower vase *iniingatang di mabasag, ang puso ng kanilang mga labandera dinudurog sa masasakit na salita.* Pope Benedict XVI in *Caritas in Veritate* said that we should learn how to combine concern for the environmental ecology with human ecology. We do not only take care only of the environment, we take care also of human beings, the apex of creation. Our attitude towards the environment influences our attitude towards human beings. Created in the image and likeness of God, human beings manifest the loving Creator in a unique way. As stewards of creation, human beings have been made to share in God's caring for His handiwork. Of all creatures, human beings are the most captivating. Unfortunately, the beauty of nature captivates some people more than the divine likeness in their neighbors. Human persons are turned into objects, commodities, specimens and functions, while other creatures are worshipped. In the process, the mystery of having been wonderfully created in the image of God is ignored or even violated.

So creation speaks, it is one voice of the Word. *At sana naman, ngayong panahon ng Ondoy at Pepeng,* creation is not just a voice leading us to prayer and adoration. Maybe, creation is also the voice of God's wrath. Paul tells us that the whole of creation is groaning as it awaits the revelation of the freedom of the children of God (Rom 8:19-23). Creation is also waiting for responsible children of God to be revealed finally. *Hindi lang tayo ang naiinip. Naiinip na rin ang* creation.

The Transmission of Revelation. The final point concerns the transmission of the Word. To be consistent with the metaphor, we can use the image of echoing the Voice of the Word. According to Hebrews 1:1, "God spoke in partial and various ways to our ancestors through the prophets. In these last days, He spoke to us through a Son, whom He made heir of all things and through whom He created the universe." The human voice of the Son gives human form to God's Word. But, the Son is the Word and the Voice. The peak of Revelation occurs when the medium and the message have become one in the sending of the Son in human flesh.

Jesus entrusted his word and teaching to his apostles and to the whole Church. *Dei Verbum* calls the bishops the authoritative interpreters of the deposit of the Word of God so that it could be passed on in its integrity and purity (DV 25). But that does not mean that only the bishops are capable of interpreting the word of God. Every member of the Church, by virtue of the common charism of the *sensus fidei*, contributes to the interpretation and transmission of Revelation. Catechists and parents, do not pass the responsibility only to the priests and to the Magisterium. It is a common responsibility. After all, the whole Church is the Body of Christ.

Testimony plays a crucial role in the transmission of the Word of God. According to *Dei Verbum,* the Word of God is one deposit (DV 10) and you find it in the written word (Scriptures) and also in Tradition. So, what do we transmit? It is not just the written word. We pass on to the next generations our whole faith and what we are as a Church. We submit to the Word and allow it to determine our values, attitudes, lifestyle and criteria for pastoral decisions. Only in our religious obedience to the Voice of God in Tradition can we become the credible witnesses to that Voice.

Ang tanong ko po: Do people still listen to the Church? Do people still listen to the voice of their pastors? What makes people—especially the young—listen? What makes them ignore our voice? What makes the young people ignore the voice of their parents, their teachers, and their Church? How deeply do we immerse ourselves in the rich Tradition so that with the chorus of voices that have constituted it from of old, we may add our own, like the wise person who draws the truth from the old and the new?

From the Voice that speaks and acts through history and creation, now we continue the history, we echo the Voice. And, we hope that through the faithful transmission of the Word of God, history will be changed and the new creation, i.e. salvation, will always be effective.

Conclusion. We try our best to be the voice for the Word of God, but how difficult it is. *Yung mga mag-asawa nga: nagsasalita ka pa, paglingon mo nakaalis na pala asawa. Mga* teachers, *nauubos yung boses mo, pagdating ng* exam *wala palang natutunan mga estudyante. Hanggang kailan tayo mananawagan ng malinis na eleksyon, nakakasawa na. Saan napunta ang mga tinig na iyan? Saan?*

To close this reflection on the Voice of the Word and to give us a little hope, I turn to John the Baptist, the voice crying out in the wilderness, calling on all to prepare for the coming of the Lord. But a voice shouting in the wilderness is a wasted voice, for no one hears. The wilderness swallows the voice into its void. The voice disappears slowly into nothingness. This is our experience too. We often feel that our voice lands on a vast emptiness. But our faith tells us that someone listens—God, the One whose voice created the world, humanity and history from a dark emptiness. God continues to speak His word, scattering the seeds of the Word, even on useless rocky and thorny ground. No voice is ever wasted for the God who desires to save, even those with stony and thorny hearts. *Magbabaka-sakali lagi ang Diyos.*

It is also interesting to note that in Mark's gospel, Jesus died with a loud cry, not with words, but with a cry. On the wilderness of the cross, we hear the voice of the humiliated, unaccepted Word. His final human word was a cry without words. Have we not all experienced this—our surrender of self into God's hand in trust and faith happening with a loud cry? This voice without words, resounding with faith, obedience, and trust is Jesus' final way of saying *"Abba."* That cry to the Father that revealed his heart, his heart that saved us, gave us the Holy Spirit who enables us also to cry out, *"Abba,* Father" (Rom 8). In the wilderness of our ministry, in the wilderness of our economy and devastation, in the wilderness of our family life, let us not fear to cry out loudly to the Father who hears in the wilderness. We hope that in our daily baptism into the baptism of Jesus leading to our own transfiguration with Jesus, we may finally hear the Voice from on high, "You are my beloved son."

The Roads of the Word: Mission

Teodoro Bacani, Jr.

Good afternoon to all of you. *Alam niyo natutuwa ako*; I realized just now that the first two speakers were my students in Loyola School of Theology. Then Father Arévalo, who will be the last speaker—we were all his students at one time or another. *Maganda*. There is an age progression.

A God Who Speaks. Let me begin by sharing a story that was told us by a missionary. This missionary had a Buddhist friend. At one time, he thought of getting his friend to know more about Christianity. And so, he said, "If you want to know more about my God, then, here read this book." He handed his friend the Bible. After a week, the Buddhist friend came to him with a frustrated and disappointed face and said, "I cannot understand your God. He is a noisy God." So the missionary asked, "Why do you say that he is a noisy God?" "Well, he keeps on speaking in this book that you gave me," the Buddhist said.

Yes, our God, the Christian God, is a God who speaks. He loves to speak to us, not because he wants to make noise. There is a poster that says "'May I talk to you?' –God." That is really our God. He wants to talk to us, not to make noise, but to make bonds with us.

From the earliest pages of the Bible God is depicted as speaking his creative word which brought about light, the earth, and all the things in it. God is pictured as talking to the first human beings, giving them stewardship of the world. He talks to Adam, and tells him that he may eat of all the fruits of the trees in the garden except of the fruit of the tree of the knowledge of good and evil, and warns him that if he does eat of the fruit of the tree of the knowledge of good and evil he would die. He calls out to Adam after his disobedience to God's command. He likewise calls out to Cain to ask him where his brother Abel is. To mark a new stage in the history of humankind, he tells Abram to leave the land of his kinsfolk to go to a land which he would show Abram. He promises to make of him a great nation.

The history of salvation is the history of God's speaking to his people not only through words but also—and perhaps, more especially—through deeds. The Letter to the Hebrews begins with these words: "In times past, God spoke in partial and various ways to our ancestors through the prophets; in these last days, he spoke to us through a son" (Heb 1:1-2). This Son is himself the Word who was with God in the beginning, and who was God like the Father, and became human, born of the Virgin Mary when the fullness of time came.

This Son, the Word become human, was the revelation of the Father and of his love. In coming into the world, he proclaimed and made real for people with the power of the Holy Spirit, the reign of God, the love and will of his Father. Glorified by his passion, death and resurrection, he gave to his disciples the Holy Spirit so that they might continue his mission as the Father had sent him. Thus, through them, Jesus wanted the Good News to be proclaimed to the whole world: "Go into the whole world and proclaim the gospel to every creature" (Mark 16:15). And from then on, the word of God, which is the word of Christ, has gone out to all the earth.

The Mission of Jesus and the Church. Jesus was

anointed for a mission of liberation: "to bring glad tidings to the poor ... to proclaim liberty to captives and recovery of sight to the blind, to let the oppressed go free, and to proclaim a year acceptable to the Lord" (Luke 4:18-19). He liberated people from the bondage of sin, calling them to repentance, forgiving sins. But, he also liberated them from sickness, possession by the devil, and death, which are consequences and manifestations of sin.

Today, the Church must preach the gospel of liberation from sin and from the consequences and manifestations of sin. Realizing that sin, while residing in the hearts of people, extends and manifests itself in social structures (habitual ways of human interaction) which have injustice built into them, the Church, through her children must not only preach repentance and the forgiveness of sins, but must also work for the reform of unjust social structures and systems that perpetuate and manifest human sinfulness. As far back as 1971, in the statement of Synod of Bishops, we find this lapidary statement: "Action on behalf of justice and participation in the transformation of the world fully appear to us as a constitutive dimension of the preaching of the Gospel" (*Justitia in Mundo* 6). Everything that the Church does—every prayer that is said, every penance that is endured, every action that is taken, every suffering that is undergone—all of this is meant also for the promotion of justice and the transformation of society.

Jesus came to enhance human life, to give us life in abundance. He came that we might become the adopted sons and daughters of God. In fact, by uniting himself to a concrete human nature, he united himself in some way with every human being, and by that very fact, human nature was in him raised to a dignity beyond compare, which he wants to share with us (*Gaudium et Spes* 22). The word of God today is meant to nourish people for eternal life, while not neglecting to preach and to strive that all human beings should have a share in this world's goods. The mission of proclaiming the word of God today must have as its purpose not only integral human liberation but integral human development, the development of each person and of all persons in all their human dimensions and according to their vocation to eternal life.

Jesus came to reconcile and unite people. He preached love of all human beings, even of our enemies. He proclaimed and demanded that we forgive our offenders even as we seek forgiveness for our offenses. He not only prayed that all his followers might become one as he and the Father are one, but he also died in order to gather together the scattered children of God.

But beyond reconciling and uniting persons with one another, he proclaimed the reign of God precisely to unite people with God. This for him was the most important thing: that people should seek first of all the kingdom of God and that they should be united to his Father by doing his will, as Jesus himself sought to always do.

The Church was established by Christ as a sacrament, that is, a sign and instrument of the intimate union of men and women with God, and the unity of all humankind (*Lumen Gentium* 1). It finds its unity first of all from the word of the living God (*Presbyterorum Ordinis* 4). This word, which unites people to God in whom they believe, also unites them as fellow believers. It is this word also, with its central message of God's love and call to reconciliation with God and with each other, which the Church seeks to bring to other people by the example of the Church's own members and by the spoken word.

It is this understanding of the mission of the Church which is enshrined in these words of the Philippine bishops (in 1977): "This is *Evangelization*: the proclamation, above all, of *salvation* from sin; the *liberation* from everything oppressive to man; the *development* of man in all his dimensions, personal and communitarian; and ultimately, the *renewal of society* in all its strata through the interplay of the *Gospel truths* and man's concrete *total life* (Pope Paul VI, *Evangelii Nuntiandi*, n. 9, 29). *This is our task. This is our mission*" [emphases in original].

The Lord Jesus, however, while urging his disciples to become the salt of the earth and the light of the world, and while depicting the kingdom of heaven as near, never restricted his vision and mission within the boundaries of this world. He spoke of the kingdom of heaven and of a future beyond this life and this world's history. There will be a future fulfillment of human life in the kingdom of God which will be fully manifested at the end of human history. It is true that "we are God's children now; what we shall be has not yet been revealed. We do know that when it is revealed we shall be like him, for we shall see him as he is" (1 John 3:2). There will come a time beyond history when all evil, even death will be conquered, and all will be submitted to God by the Lord, and "God will be all in all" (1 Cor 15:28). Jesus taught us to pray for that time when he taught us to pray, "Our Father ... thy kingdom come."

Hence, the mission of the Church, the proclamation of the Word of God will always seek to help people to hope for that future known only to God, when our lives and the universe itself will find their consummation, and where we shall finally inhabit new heavens and a new earth where the justice of God shall dwell (2 Pet 3:13). Consistent with this, the Second Plenary Council of the Philippines [PCP-II] declares that "evangelization and salvation evidently cannot be identified with nor be reduced to a task of temporal liberation" (242).

The Unsettling Dimension of Evangelization. Up to now I am quite sure that I have said nothing particularly unsettling. The proclamation of the word of God, the mission of evangelization seems to be a non-threatening and tranquilizing reality. But the kind of death that Jesus' preaching of the word of God led to and the long trail of the blood of martyrs from ancient times to the present should already hint at the non-tranquil nature of evangelization. Jesus' preaching of the Good News led him to death by crucifixion, and he invited those who wished to follow him to be ready to also suffer the same fate for the sake of the gospel. What is so dangerous or threatening about preaching the Good News of the Kingdom of God, the Good News of God's love, and the personification of this Good News in Jesus Christ, the Savior of the world?

The answer lies in the phrase used by Pope Paul VI and the Philippine bishops when they speak of evangelization as involving the interplay of the Gospel truths and humanity's concrete total life.

The Gospel truths which express the values of Christ and of God will inevitably come into conflict with much of what people and those who are powerful or matter in society hold dear. Hence, to proclaim these Gospel truths in the concrete situation of a given group will entail also a critique and resistance against what people and the powerful of this world cherish and must protect. Pope Paul VI in *Evangelii Nuntiandi*, states plainly that the Church "seeks by virtue of the gospel to affect, and, as it were, recast the criteria of judgment, the standard of values, the incentives and life standards of the human race which are inconsistent with the word of God and the plan of salvation" (EN 19). The Church (though not a habitual fault-finder) will always find something in any society that falls short of the standards of the Kingdom of God, and the Gospel of her Lord Jesus Christ.

Indeed, it is true that "evangelizing means above all else the bearing witness simply and clearly to God as he is revealed by Our Lord Jesus Christ, proclaiming that he has loved the world in his Son and that in the Incarnate Word he has given existence to all creatures and has called them to eternal life" (EN 26). "But evangelization will not be complete unless it constantly relates the gospel to men's actual lives, personal and social. Accordingly, evangelization must include an explicit message, adapted to the various conditions of life and constantly updated, concerning the rights and duties of the individual person and concerning family life.... It must deal with community life in society, with the life of all nations, with peace, justice, and progress. It must deliver a message, especially relevant and important in our age, about liberation" (EN 29).

In many countries and in the Philippines, there are people "striving with all their power and energy to overcome all those circumstances which compel them to live on the border line of existence: hunger, chronic epidemics, illiteracy, poverty, injustice between nations and especially in the commercial sphere, economic and cultural neo-colonialism, which are often as bad as the old political colonialism." And so, "The Church is duty bound ... to proclaim the liberation of these hundred of millions of people since very many of them are her children. She has the duty of helping this liberation, of bearing witness on its behalf and of assuring its full development" (EN 30).

If one understands the preaching of the gospel in this way, then it is understandable why our Lord said that he did not come to bring peace but the sword. The Church, in proclaiming the Word in the context of an oppressive political or economic regime, will inevitably collide with powerful interests. PCP-II, in opting to be the "Church of the Poor," recognized that defending the rights of the poor may mean alienation or persecution from the rich and the powerful (131). The oppressors will often try to get the Church to their side or will at least endeavor to neutralize the influence of the Church by favors or by threats which can be very subtle. But, if she is going to be true to the tradition of the prophets and the example of the Lord, the Church must defend the poor and the oppressed by speaking out the truth and unmasking lies. That, I submit, is not a very peaceful endeavor. Right away, you get, as a minimum reaction, shouts of "separation of Church and State" saying, "Preach to us the pure Gospel, do not preach to us about human affairs of which you know nothing."

In the Philippines, what would such an understanding of evangelization entail? It means first of all, a Bible-based, Christo-centric, and systematic catechesis which will lead the faithful to know Jesus Christ, his teachings and his Church. It is a sad fact, but we must admit that the multitudes of our common faithful suffer from massive religious ignorance. There is much truth to the claim that we have been Christianized but have not been evangelized. A renewed catechesis is the first requirement of a renewed evangelization.

PCP-II pointed out that renewal in catechesis cannot stand alone. The education in the faith of our people must include a renewed social apostolate and a renewed worship. These are the three pillars, so to say, or a renewed evangelization. They support each other and include each other, and not much progress can be made in any of the three unless the other two also progress. What catechesis proclaims, the social apostolate must illustrate and confirm, and worship must energize and celebrate. The social apostolate on the other hand must be motivated by catechetical teaching and also be energized and celebrated by a life of renewed worship. This last must in turn be underpinned by solid catechetical teaching and the works of the social apostolate which it celebrates and prays for. This is what PCP-II means by integral evangelization.

Call for Inculturation of the Gospel. Evangelization, to be true and effective must be inculturated. Inculturation is "the intimate transformation of authentic cultural values through their integration in Christianity and the insertion of Christianity in the various human cultures" (*Redemptoris Missio* 52). The process of inculturation will demand a truly Filipino way of presenting the message to Filipinos. But, the insertion of the Gospel in our culture will affect and upset our culture's "criteria of judgment, determining values, points of interest, lines of thought, sources of inspiration and models of life which are in contrast with the Word of God and the plan of salvation" (EN 19). In other words—if I may use a more provocative word—inculturation will have to be subversive. The Gospel will not always give a nod of assent to what are propagated daily by the mass media, our economic systems and political culture. Inculturation, because it entails the purification of cultures by the Gospel values, will necessary entail tension and conflict with those who profit from the cultural status quo. It is only through inculturation, however, that our culture will be evangelized. Without inculturation, the Christian message will be passed on as religious information, but it will *not* touch the heart, move the will to act, and transform our life and culture.

Let me give an illustration of what happens when we inculturate. Remember the parable told by the Lord in the Gospel of Luke (12:16-21) about the rich man who had a bumper harvest. The rich man felt very secure since he thinks he had all things in life, and so he says, "What will I do? This is what I will do. I have enough for myself. I shall eat, drink, and be merry for I have enough for a lifetime. I will just build bigger barns, and that is it." And God said to him, "*You fool. This day they will demand your soul from you.*"

One day, I tried the following during a Mass in Paco. I read the Gospel as it was in the Lectionary. I translated what the Lord said to the rich man. The Lord said to him: *"Gago!"* See, when I said "You fool," you did not react at all. But when I said *"Gago,"* you reacted. *Iba kasi ang dating ng "Gago!" sa "You fool!"* *Tinuloy ko pa, "Tignan ninyo, marami palang gago—naka-Mercedes Benz, nakatira sa mga* exclusive villages, *kumakain sa masasarap na restawran, tumutuloy sa magagandang hotel—pero gago pa rin."* After the Mass, somebody told me, "Bishop *naman, yung* language *mo, iingatan mo."* I think that person would have to try approaching Jesus and say the same thing. *Ang mangyayari* English *na, kaya kapag sinabi sa ating,* "You fool," *baka sabihin lang natin,* "Thank you." *Iba talaga, may kagat kapag sinabing, "Gago."* That is what inculturation does. It makes you feel it. You will feel the Gospel in the guts, your stomach moves. And hopefully, it will move you. Inculturation is essential. Otherwise, the Good News will not hit you with the full force and energy that it has; it has been enervated already, deprived of its strength.

Evangelization as it is now understood by the Church entails the evangelization of culture and of cultures. In the Philippines it involves necessarily the evangelization of our economic and political culture. The two are intertwined. Lack of time constrains me to speak of the transformation of our political culture. Politics, which is the noble art of promoting organized action for the common good, has so badly degenerated in our country that as it is practiced today, it is probably the greatest obstacle to our integral development as a nation. Our political system is so riddled by corruption that corruption (according to the CBCP again) has become our national shame. It is even more shameful because we are the biggest Catholic country in Asia. Unless our politics is fixed correctly, we will fail to give a shining witness to our contemporaries in this part of the world.

Think, dear brothers and sisters, what inculturation means for our culture so riddled corruption, greed, and deceitfulness in politics and business. It will require not only knowledge and sensitivity to our culture but the prophetic courage to denounce what is contrary to the word of God. True inculturation requires boldness from the evangelizer, the boldness (*parrhesia*) that characterizes the disciples in the Acts of the Apostles. Gregory the Great said, "Pastors who lack foresight hesitate to say openly what is right because they fear losing the favor of men. As the voice of truth tells us, such leaders are not zealous pastors who protect their flock. Rather, they are mercenaries who flee by taking refuge in silence when the wolf appears. When the pastor has been afraid to assert what is right, has he not turned his back and fled by remaining silent?"

Fully aware of our sad situation, PCP-II made it clear that one of the goals of evangelization is the transformation of Philippine society. But to transform Philippine society, we have to transform Philippine politics by evangelizing it. But transforming politics cannot be done unless there is a moral regeneration of our people. What is needed to transform Philippine politics is not only a change of political structures or of leaders but a change in people, in their hearts. In the Philippines, that change of heart must derive its grace from and be patterned after the hearts of Jesus and Mary, two hearts that beat in unison with love for God and love for people, two hearts inflamed with a passion for God and compassion for people, especially the poor. Hence the year from June 2009 to June 2010, the year for prayer and action for peace and social change has been placed by our bishops under the patronage of the Sacred Heart of Jesus and the Immaculate Heart of Mary.

Also, a most timely aspect of evangelization now is that which is for the transformation of environment. Let me just propose five principles that can serve as a sort of syllabus for this kind of evangelization. First, this world and our selves are gifts from God, from his gratuitousness. Second, this world of ours is God's home. Third, it is our home. Fourth, our mandate is to use this world and develop and care for it, not abuse and waste it. And fifth, the way we treat the world is the way the world will treat us.

New Methods, New Expressions, New Fervor. When Pope John Paul II called for a new evangelization, he called for "new methods, new expressions, and new fervor" (*Pastores Dabo Vobis* 18). Let me say a few brief words on "new methods." Witness is a method that remains perennially new. "Modern man listens more to witnesses than to teachers," said Pope Paul VI, and "if he listens to teachers, it is because they are also witnesses" (EN 41). The recent death and massive expression of gratitude shown by our people on the occasion of the death and funeral of President Cory Aquino illustrated this. Our people showed that they were affected deeply by the Christian witness of a woman who used political power not for herself but for the people, a person who could remain incorrupt while holding the highest political position in the land.

What has emerged also is the need "to come together, to pray together, to discuss together, to decide together and to act together," a method first proposed by the CBCP in its Post-Snap Election Statement in 1985, and repeated on other occasions. Recently too, "circles of discernment" have been proposed and practiced as a way of bringing about political change. Such a method is a particular realization of the dialogical mode of evangelization proposed by the 1974 FABC Plenary Assembly held in Taipei: dialogue with the people, especially the poor; dialogue with local cultures; and, dialogue with other religious traditions. What is coming out now is the need to see evangelization not as a handing on only of doctrine but as a participative and dialogical process by which the good news is transmitted and personally accepted.

In discussing evangelization, the multifaceted process of presenting the Word of God, we cannot neglect mention of the mass media and the many modern means of communication which speedily hand on any word and any news, and have made our world not only a global village but a global house.

The modern means of communication have made our task both easier and more challenging. We have these means at our disposal and neglect them to our own harm and befriend them for our good. Modern evangelizers should be media friendly and media literate. We should use the technology with artistry and persuasiveness. We should invest in them wisely. Can we present the word of God and our Christian values as attractively as our *telenovelas* have been presenting their stories?

I hope that you gather by now that the work of bringing to others God's word, the Good News, must necessarily harness the energies of our lay faithful. The renewal of our families, the renewal of our society, the renewal of politics will need the participation and involvement of our Christian lay faithful. No one of them should be content to only be evangelized. Each must in turn, and with others become an evangelizer. It is through the lay faithful that the word of God becomes effectively salt of the earth and light of the world, leaven for this world's transformation.

All this has already become a reality in that aspect of mission which is a complement of the mission within our country—which I have been mostly speaking about. I am speaking of mission "without," "beyond," the mission of bringing the word of God to those who do not yet believe. It is true we already have several thousands of priests and religious sisters and brothers serving as missionaries in the *missio ad gentes* which must remain a top priority. But, we already have millions of lay faithful in non-Christian lands, or in once-Christian lands, whom providence has placed as advance forces of evangelization. Through them God's word can be proclaimed, and even more importantly take flesh in the countries where economic necessity may have brought them. As in days of old, the Good News was spread by common people, by traders and even by slaves, so today too the seeds of the Word can be spread by our Filipino overseas workers and migrants, more than eight million strong.

Loving the Gospel, the Gospel of Love. I will conclude not by summarizing what I have been saying thus far, but by underlining the most important element of mission, which is charity. As mission originated from the fountain of love which is God, and as the message that we bring is "God so loved the world that he gave his only Son so that we may have life everlasting through him" (John 3:16), so too, the most important element of a renewed evangelization is what Pope John Paul II termed "a new fervor," and which Pope Paul VI had described before him as "the fervor of the saints." Charity, or love, is the soul of the apostolate and of all mission. As Saint Therese of the Child Jesus discovered long ago, nothing would come out and nothing would be done unless the fire of love moved the apostles, confessors, doctors and martyrs to their deeds. We must draw this love from the Holy Spirit, nurture it through study and meditation on the Word of God, nourish it through the Eucharist, and cultivate it through community living. The Word of God will make its way to the hearts of men and women, to the homes of families and to communities of men, women and children, and renew the face of the earth if it is carried in the hearts, proclaimed by the lips, and incarnated in the lives of evangelizers who are aflame with love and are urged by the charity of Christ to give their lives, even if there be a thousand of them, for God and for the faith.

Saint Gregory the Great said, "Because I love Him, I have not spared myself in speaking of him." And so, when we have that love that inflames the hearts of witnesses, we will never spare ourselves in speaking and bearing witness to our Lord Jesus Christ.

Reflections on the Word of God: A Synthesis

Catalino C. Arévalo

It is hard to say what we are supposed to do for a synthesis, so let me just try my best, in just summing up a few points. Both Bishop Tagle and Bishop David indicated in their talks the overall outline of what is called the *Nuntius* or the Message of the Synod of 2008. They had four major headings: the Voice of the Word—Revelation, the Face of the Word—Jesus Christ, the House of the Word—Church, and the Roads of the Word—Mission. Now, it is hard to see how we can synthesize, because all of the talks were already syntheses.

When they are preparing for a Synod, the first document that comes out is the *Lineamenta*, a kind of an overall outline of the theme that is distributed to all the bishops for their study and discussion and their feedback. The second step is to make what is called the working paper, the *Instrumentum Laboris*, that becomes the immediate preparation for the discussions. Then, the discussions take place in the Synod during the assembly. Finally, the pope will come out with a document called an Apostolic Exhortation that sums up the fruits of the Synod discussions.

Revisiting the Themes. Let me just pick up some points from Bishop Tagle's paper; I will be very selective. Firstly, the Word of God is a voice spoken and an event done. The voice reveals the content of the heart and the soul and reveals the very identity of the person. And then, the identity of the speaker and its effect on the listener is performative, effective, and dynamic. It is transformative and shapes history. Now, one thing that we need to point out here is that the Catholic view of the word of God is that it is not just a book. This is absolutely normative in the Catholic understanding of the Word. When we say the word of God, we go way beyond the book to the events: first, to the events of salvation history, which are narrated in the book, but ultimately, as we shall see, to the Christ event, the person of the Lord, the person who was Jesus Christ is the Word. I would like to insist on this, because for the Catholic understanding of scripture, it is very important to understand that ultimately what we mean by the word of God is the person of Christ himself, not the book. We go beyond the book to the events of salvation history and we go beyond simply the events of salvation history to the person of Christ.

There is a shaping of history that comes from the word, and, as Bishop Tagle pointed out, from this we see the role of the prophets. The prophets reveal to people the inner meaning of events, God's intention in the events of history. Thus, from the words is revealed the mind of God, and people discover the meaning of their lives. Both the synod message and the pope are constantly saying that that is in some true sense the ultimate purpose of reading the Word. We read the Word to discover in the ongoing history of ourselves, our peoples, and the world, the meaning of our lives, as individuals, communities, and peoples in the light of faith. The prophets of every age reveal to people what their lives, in their ups and downs, in their light and darkness, joy and pain mean and their relation to the law of the Paschal mystery.

Bishop Tagle also took up the theme of the transmission of revelation. Revelation is transmitted primarily through the apostolic witness, that is, the teaching of the apostles and of the apostolic Church. It is the Spirit who teaches and speaks to us when we read and reflect on the Word. And, the Spirit speaks to us as a people first of all. The Word is put in a book of a people for the sake of a people. It is not an individual book; even when the individual Christian reads the Bible, he reads it as a message to the entire people not just to himself. Therefore as we shall see, within the Catholic understanding of the scripture, there is always the community. The book is for the community. It is the community who reads the book. That is what we mean by Tradition. The book lives within the community.

That community is the Church, which was the theme of the talk of Bishop David. At the beginning, he took us through a biblically based journey from the temple of Jerusalem as a house of fire, which in time ran out of the fire of mercy and compassion. When that house became empty of the divine fire and the people of God were dispersed and exiled, they rediscovered the Word. After they had lost the holy city and the temple, it was the Word which became the center of the life of the holy people. While in exile they had the Word, the Torah, around which they gathered in synagogues and hoped again. Of course, that hope is fulfilled finally in Jesus.

Then Bishop David brought us back into the *Nuntius* which says that the Church, as the home of the Word, is built on four pillars that are mentioned in Acts 2:42: "They devoted themselves to the instruction of the apostles and the community life, the fellowship, to the breaking of the bread and prayers." The first pillar is the *didache*, the apostolic teaching today, which involves preaching, catechesis and especially, for the *Nuntius*, the homily. For very many Catholics, we hope that this is being remedied at the present time.

The contact with the scripture is primarily through the liturgy and the homily. The homily is not meant to be just a question of stories and so on. It is supposed to be the one weekly time when the people are put in contact with the meaning of the Word of God. The present pope continually warns priests that the homily is not for saying your own words, but for bringing the meaning of the word of God into the lives of the people every Sunday. It is supposed to help them each Sunday to deepen the Christian understanding of the meaning of their lives. People are beginning to realize this more and more. I hear now of people traveling even from the provinces every Sunday to go to churches where they will not just to listen to cute stories and jokes, but to a homily that will help them to go deeper into the very meaning of their lives and their Christian vocation.

The second pillar of the Church as the house of the word is the breaking of the bread. Notice, this comes from the Acts of the Apostles. Already during that time, the breaking of the bread is an essential part of the house of the Word. The Eucharist and the Scripture are together; they are not to be separated. The Eucharist is the supreme work of the Word who offers himself as food in the immolated body of Christ, the source and summit of the life and mission of the Church (*Sacrosanctum Concilium* 10).

The third pillar is the prayers: psalms, hymns and inspired songs as called for by Paul in Colossians 3:16. The *Nuntius* says that today that is largely the Liturgy of the Hours, which unfortunately is just known to priests and religious. But in many churches both in Europe and in the States, the liturgy of the hours is being shared much more with lay people.

Last is *koinonia*, the fellowship, the communal life, the fraternal life, the witnessing to the word of God in life and deed. The Message says that *koinonia* includes all our brothers and sisters in the community of faith and it reaches out to other Christian Churches and communities. There can be no communion with Christ Jesus in a gathering where the members despise one another and have no communion with one another.

Notice that both Bishop Tagle and Bishop David are pointing out things which are part of the Catholic reading of the Scriptures: that it is always within the Church. Very recently when I gave a talk to one of the dioceses, one of the main problems facing the parishes is that very few Catholics know how to read the Scriptures in a Catholic way. When they want to learn how to read the Scriptures, they bring in Protestant biblical experts or teachers. Thus, the problem that faces many communities is that the people who do read the Scriptures in the parishes are reading it in a Protestant way. I am not criticizing the Protestant way, but there is a Catholic way of reading the Scriptures and it is always within the life of the Church.

You just heard Bishop Bacani on Mission: the roads of the word. I will not even try to summarize it here because as usual with him, it is always a brief but integral presentation. When Bishop Bacani presents, all the essential elements are touched on, and touched on briefly and clearly. But, he did not take up the *Nuntius,* and he developed the notion of mission of the Church as the roads of the Word referring primarily to *Evangelii Nuntiandi,* that document of Paul VI following the Synod on Evangelization in 1974. His biographers consider this document as one of his best, and Bishop Bacani shows how relevant and up to date that document still is. He links it up also with the Second Plenary Council of the Philippines [PCP II], and at the end—something which I think is rather valuable—he links it up with the Year of the Two Hearts. We do not have the time to develop that. Those are the only points that I thought I would stress a little bit for you to remember.

Filling up a Lacuna. Let me go to one part in the *Nuntius* which was not assigned to anybody: the Face of the

Word, the Person of Jesus. In a sense this is the most important thing and I am little surprised that not one whole talk was given to it (although Bishop Tagle mentions it). Let me fill up a little bit that lacuna, that hole as it were.

The Message says that the three words "*Logos sarx eghéneto*" from the prologue of the Gospel of John (1:14) is the actual heart of the Christian faith and of the Church.

> The eternal and divine Word enters into space and time and takes on a human face and identity, so much so that it is possible to approach him directly asking, as did the group of Greeks present in Jerusalem, "We would like to see Jesus" (John 12:20-21). Words without a face are not perfect, they do not fully complete the encounter, as Job recalled, reaching the end of his dramatic itinerary of searching, "Before, I knew you only by hearsay. But now I have seen you with my own eyes" (Job 42:5) [*Nuntius* 4].

The point here is that, again, everything points to the person of Christ. When we say the Word of God, we do not say primarily the book, we mean primarily the person of Christ. The book points and leads to the person of Christ. Now, the *Nuntius* has some very important paragraphs which I would like to share with you.

> Here thus lies the necessity of the "living Tradition of all the Church" (DV 12) and of the faith to understand Sacred Scripture in a full and unified way. Should one focus only on the "letter," the Bible is only a solemn document of the past, a noble, ethical and cultural witness. If, however, the Incarnation is excluded, it could fall into a funda-mentalist equivocation or a vague spiritualism or pop-psychology. Exegetical knowledge must,

therefore, weave itself indissolubly with spiritual and theological tradition so that the divine and human unity of Jesus Christ and Scripture is not broken [*Nuntius* 6].

The pope insists that the word of God is alive now. It is speaking to us now. It is not a book who is speaking to us. It is the living Jesus, through the Spirit, who speaks to us when we read the book.

In this rediscovered harmony, the face of Christ will shine in its fullness and will help us to discover another unity, that profound and intimate unity of the Sacred Scriptures [*Nuntius* 6].

We do not read the Scriptures in little bits and pieces separated from each other. The seventy three books of the Scriptures are one book. The danger of the critical exegesis and critical study of the Bible at the present time is that, instead of the Bible being one book, it is separated into little passages: this passage came from here; that passage came from there; this passage is influenced by this; that passage was influenced by that; this passage means this; that passage means that. But, we read further,

The seventy three books are for the Catholic reading of Scriptures one book from Genesis to Revelation; and every book helps to interpret every part of every other book. They form only one "Canon," one dialogue between God and humanity, one plan of salvation. "In times past God spoke in partial and diverse ways to our ancestors through the prophets. In these last days, he spoke to us in the person of his Son" (Heb 1:1). Christ thus retrospectively sheds his light on the entire development of salvation history and reveals its coherence, meaning, and direction. He is the seal, "the Alpha and the Omega" (Rev 1:8) of a dialogue between God and his creatures distributed over time and attested to in the Bible. It is in the light of this final seal that the words of Moses and the prophets acquire their "full sense." Jesus himself had indicated this on that spring afternoon, while he made his way from Jerusalem to the town of Emmaus, dialoguing with Cleopas and his friend, explaining "to them the passages in the Scriptures that were about himself" (Luke 24:27). That the divine Word has put on a face is at the center of Revelation. That is precisely why the ultimate finality of biblical knowledge is "not the result of an ethical choice or a lofty idea, but the encounter with an event, a person, which gives life a new horizon and a decisive direction" (*Deus Caritas Est* 1) [*Nuntius* 6].

The whole purpose of the reading, study, and meditation of the Bible and of the contemplation of what it means in our lives, is to constantly encounter Christ. I read in a book not too long ago something about a church in New York in the old days, when there was still a pulpit. When the preacher was going up to the pulpit, he finds written on its door the words that we quoted from the Gospel of John: "Sir, we would like to see Jesus." So when the preacher goes up to the pulpit, he knows the purpose why he is there. He wants to answer the demand, the desire of the people who say, "Sir, we would like to see Jesus."

The *Nuntius* says that the Bible, is also, therefore and primarily, flesh. It is human in so many ways. The Bible, just as the Son of God, became flesh and became one of us. As *Dei Verbum* quotes Saint Ambrose, "For the words of God expressed in human words have been made like human language just as the word of the eternal father when it took on himself the flesh of human weakness became man" (*Dei Verbum* 13). The

Son of God took on human flesh and became just like us in so many ways. He became a particular person, in a particular time and a particular place, speaking a particular language and wearing particular clothes. When you become flesh, you become particularized. So, the Bible is the same thing; the word of God becomes incarnate in definite words of a definite language, culture, and period in history. Divine inspiration does not erase historicity and the particularities of the human authors. Thus, the *Nuntius* says, there is need of a scientific understanding of the Bible (although the word "scientific" is not used) through what we call biblical exegesis. We cannot be fundamentalists. The Scriptures must be decoded, studied and understood by us who live in a completely different culture, time, and circumstance.

Also, because one is human, you need the inspiration of the Spirit so that the words of Scripture are not just human words, but they are the Word of God, the divine Word which gives us the divine mind, the divine intent, and the divine meaning. Here thus lies the need of the living tradition of the Church. The book cannot be read outside of a living tradition of the Church. You need faith to read it, to understand the Scriptures in a complete and unified way.

Let me sum up what was said thus far. That the divine word has put on a face is at the center of revelation. The ultimate finality of biblical knowledge is not the result of an ethical choice, not a code of morality, nor of lofty ideas. It is not a combination of religious ideas. The whole purpose of the word of God, of the reading of the Scriptures is a living encounter with an event, a person which gives to life a new horizon and a decisive direction. I thought that would be good for us to remember. There is a Catholic way of reading the Scriptures. And, this Catholic way is precisely what we have just said. It must lead to the living person of Christ. The moment you make the Bible a book of the past and just sort of understanding the past, you are no longer reading the Bible in a Catholic way.

Benedict XVI on the Word of God. The present pope continually comes back to this [we refer to this in the document on the Year of the Two Hearts]. What did Jesus actually come to do in this world? The pope says he did not come to make it a better world; the world today is probably worse than it was in the time of Jesus. Nor did Jesus come to bring material prosperity to humanity; there are more poor people and suffering people now than ever in the history of humanity. Nor did he come to create a perfect society; our society today is probably much worse than the society where Jesus lived. So what did Jesus come to do? The pope tells us that he came to give us God. That too is the specific purpose of the Church and of the Christian. It is not to make a better world, create a prosperous society, or bring about world peace. That is the duty of every human being: man, woman and child. But, the specific purpose of the Church is to constantly bring in God as Jesus did.

Today, the pope says, many Christians do not want to speak about God. Many priests will talk only about politics and about values, society, truth, justice and so on. They will not speak about God. We have now come to a secularized time, when even priests are afraid to speak of God. He says that is wrong. Our purpose, if we are Christians, is to bring God into everything. Values, correct institutions, truth, justice are all good things and are the concerns of every human being in this world. But the specific concern of the Christian Church is the concern of Jesus which is to bring in God, to bring in the Word of God. And our purpose as Christians, in the body of Christ, is to bring Christ into the world. Our reading of the Scriptures is that massive gift to us from God so that we can be constantly guided in understanding the meaning of Jesus.

In the homily that the pope gave at the end of the Synod on the Word of God, he tried to sum up in about fifteen minutes what the whole Synod was all about [the present pope is a perfect example of how to take the Word of God and apply it to our time]. He recalled how an expert of the law came to Jesus and asked for one formula that will sum up the entire Scriptures—the law and the prophets, the one unifying principle in the various ways that God and God's will is spoken about in the Bible. There are six hundred and thirteen precepts and prohibitions regarding the doing of God's will in the Hebrew Bible, but Jesus answers without hesitation citing the *Shema*, the prayer recited by pious Jews several times a day: "You shall love the Lord your God with all your heart, with all your soul and with all your mind" (Deut 6:4-5). Jesus insists on the total and integral dedication of the person to God and it involves the three main faculties of man that constitute his deep psychological structures: sentiment (the heart), will (the soul) and rationality (the mind). The pope insists especially that the rationality is part of loving God. We must use our minds (*dianoia*) in loving God.

Then Jesus adds something that the questioner was not asking. He goes forward and says the second is like to the first: "You must love your neighbor as you love yourself" (Lev 19:18). This is a surprising element because Jesus sets up a parallelism between the two, and eventually says that this parallelism is really a unity. He sets up *una relazione di somiglianza* between two precepts, one key principle on which all of the biblical revelation rests. On these two commandments, the whole law and the prophets are based. The pope, in his final homily, says that if you want to sum up all of the Scriptures, Jesus himself summed it up in those two great commandments, which become in a sense one. Referring to Paul's letter to the Thessalonians, he says that every Christian community must learn that the love of neighbor is born from an attentive and docile listening to the word. How important it is then to listen to the word and to incarnate it, to embody it in one's personal existence and in the life of the community. Again, the word of God cannot be separated from the love of our brothers and sisters. If we separate them, one is sheer pietism and the other one does not derive its power and inspiration from God and the Paschal Mystery.

At the end of the Synod, the pope says that he hopes that what the bishops learned and gained is the renewed awareness that the Church's principal task, at the start of the new millennium, is above all to nourish ourselves on the word of God in order to make the new evangelization more effective in our day. We have to immerse ourselves in the word of God in order to proclaim again the meaning of life. Václav Havel says that the majority of humanity today does not know the meaning of life. But, he says, that is not bad enough. What is worse is that the vast amount of humanity does not care that it does not know the meaning of life. The purpose of reading the Scriptures is to know the meaning of life for us, which is known only in the living encounter with the person of Jesus Christ.

Where does this happen, he finally asks in the last part. For most of us, it happens in the liturgy. The liturgy is where most of us Catholics are supposed to meet the Word of God, for there is an unbreakable bond between the Word of God and the Eucharist.

Every Sunday, I go to the parish of Father Bong Tupino, Our Lady of Pentecost Parish. They have a very beautiful church. If you have not seen it, you should. What is beautiful is that, everybody in the church has a direct of view of the altar. And the priest sees absolutely everybody in the church. For a while, I used to make this kind of game for myself. I would sit down when the readings finally begin and start counting the number of people coming in during the readings. I counted sixty eight to seventy three every Sunday. Our people do not bother with the word of God. I said this to one of the parishioners, and he said, "Father, you should feel flattered. Most people come in during the homily."

Somehow, we have communicated, or the people themselves have communicated to each other, that the first part is just *habla*, not worth going to, not important. The important thing for them is the consecration. Some cars pass in front just before the Our Father; the people come out, go to Communion, then go away. This is one of the best parishes in the diocese. It is a wonderful parish. I do not say the majority of the people do this. But, we meet the word of God, the majority of Catholics specially, only during the liturgy. So I ask the people, *anong nangyayari*? *Sabi nila*, Father *yung ibang mga pari, pakwento-kwento, papogi-pogi*. They do not prepare their homilies. They do not communicate the word of God. They speak mostly about themselves.

That is why the pope has given a "general OK" for priests to face the other side again, not towards the people, at least during the Eucharistic prayer. He will not oblige everybody to do that. One of the reasons he says is that many priests have made the Eucharist a *"pogi* place" for themselves. His point is that it is in the liturgy that most Catholics meet the Scriptures. Therefore, it becomes one of the primary tasks of the priest and the people there present to make sure that the liturgy speaks the Word.

Conclusion: Mary, Our Model of Hearing and Doing the Word. Mary, then, is the model of listening to the Word, making it her own, living it through words and deeds. We have two great quotations from Our Lady about the Word. First, "Let it be done to me according to your word" (Luke 1:38), which our pope, then Joseph Ratzinger, says is the summary of the meaning of Christian sacrifice; it says "Let me open my heart so that the Word may come in and I will follow the word in my heart." We must know the Word and insert it in our lives. We must make it the source of meaning in our lives. And, the second statement is "Do whatever he tells you" (John 2:5). The word is not just received, it is also done.

So I end with that as a kind of summary of what we are to take from our reflections on the Word of God: the two words of Mary which are to lead us in our Christian life. With those, I hope that today's reflections have been useful for you and that you come from this seminar of San Jose Seminary with a longing desire to really immerse yourself in the Word of God within the life of the Church, but then, above all, to live it, in gestures of love and charity toward God and our brothers and sisters. Thank you.

Part Three

Complementary Insights from the *Verbum Dei* Forum

Four Contributions

Opening Remarks . . .

The Word of God and Priestly Spirituality

Gaudencio Cardinal Rosales

Excellencies Bishop Chito and Bishop Ambo, Father Ben Nebres and members of the academic community of this University, our rector Father Vic de Jesus, priests, seminarians, religious, brothers and sisters in Christ, good morning. I was given this space of time and I welcome this slot given to me. I also have to leave soon, because I have a date with the volunteers working in *Caritas* in Pandacan for the typhoon victims. Anyway, I am happy to be with you, to listen, to be inspired. I just listened to Bishop Ambo, but I will miss the talk of Bishop Chito, and I will not be able to listen to Father Ben.

I was also asked to come in my soutana, and I was happy when I saw Bishop Chito and Bishop Ambo in soutana. I wonder what Bishop Ted is going to wear this afternoon. But in San Jose, we take orders. The Jesuits taught us how to take it—biting your lip. That is the way it is up to now.

Secondly, I really thought I would only be talking to priests and seminarians. At least, that was the tenor of the letter of invitation. And so, sisters and lay friends, please do not be dis-edified by the way I will talk. I will address the priests and seminarians present, keeping in mind that the Holy Father declared this year as the Year for Priests. But, I will try to link it with the exhortation we have just heard.

Verbum Dei is still looking for a home. More than that, the *Verbum Dei* is looking for an expression. The *Verbum* found it once in a decision from eternity. The *Verbum* found its expression in what we are all trying to imitate and emulate in our priesthood: *Verbum caro factum est*. Finally, it found an expression that we could accept, take, treasure, live, and bring with us: Jesus.

A theologian once said that Christianity does not so much consist in a striving to be good; it is more a striving to become God. And, this is not just a mere saying, because the Good Book tells us in the first chapter of its first book that God made humans in his image and likeness. "In the image of God, He created them ... male and female he made them" (Gen 1:27). This explains why beyond being good, there is in every human person a striving for God.

Seeking God is best described by people who have lost or missed him. Having experienced not only dissatisfaction and failure, but also complete restlessness without God was best described by Saint Augustine: "But if the desire was infused in human beings to seek for God, we ask, how was God described now as reaching out to us?"

God even wanted humans to represent him, but this did not turn out the way God intended creation and humans to be. Planning from all eternity was perfect, but living the designs of God in time was another thing—it was full of mistakes. The great intervention of God in the history of humans is the introduction of his Word. God introduced his Word no longer to be spoken, not just to be preached, but as lived in Jesus, his Son, the Christ.

Et Verbum caro factum est—that was the tremendous decision of the eternal love of God that had incalculable repercussions in the unveiling of the mystery of the timeless divine love as touching our lives. From then on, the Word would be seen in as many aspects as human lives, deeds, trials, triumphs and failures would suggest. And, this is the reason why, in this forum, we are about listen to the varied reflections on what the Word of God, incarnate in Jesus, has to offer and to address to us priests and also seminarians, lay people and religious.

Where does this bring us? This brings us to our humanity, our *caro*, which remains not only weak and breakable, but actually broken. I remember once discussing with someone who insisted that the spirituality of the priest is that of the earthen vessel. I disagreed in that discussion and said "No." I believe our spirituality as priests is one of brokenness and therefore has its heart in the Paschal mystery, its finality in the experience of the cross (*Pastores Dabo Vobis* [PDV] 13). It is not just about being breakable. Earthen vessels (if you look at it) may last for centuries without breaking. But, if we are talking about the Paschal mystery, the vessels, which we are, are not just breakable; we are broken. All of us priests, religious, lay people, even the pope—we are all broken. "Unless the grain of wheat shall fall to the ground and die [be broken], it shall not bear the fruit of eternal life" (John 12:24). We are many times a shattered narrative!

The *Verbum* in the Incarnation is not just telling us a story; it reveals to us to what extent and to what depth an all-loving God can go in order to assure us of his love, in us where it resides, and for us for whom it was intended—no matter what remains of our own personal history. Let the *Verbum* touch the *caro*. Let us not preach as if we have not been broken. We had to be broken.

Verbum caro factum est. The theologian Cardinal Hans Urs von Balthasar considered this as the decision that brought the greatest humiliation to God—if God could ever be humiliated. It was in his humanity that the Incarnate Son of God, Jesus, was able to touch and assume the weaknesses and failures of all humans.

The *caro* has an important role in our salvation. It has to partner with the *Verbum*. *Verbum caro factum est.* As Tertullian puts it, "Let us see the particular relationship of the flesh in Christianity. How greatly privileged this worthless, sordid substance is, because we can say that it is impossible for the soul to obtain salvation unless it comes to faith while it is still in the flesh. *Caro salutis est cardo.*" The flesh is the hinge (*cardo*) of salvation. All the weakness and brokenness in that *caro* must be touched by the *Verbum* or else it cannot be healed, it cannot be saved. This gave rise, of course, to the theological axiom in Christology which says, "*Quod non est assumptum, non est sanatum.*" What is not assumed by the *Verbum*, cannot be healed.

Then we ask: where are we now? Given the circumstances today—ethical relativism in sexuality, the new total materialism, spiritual abandon nearly everywhere today, I believe there is reason for the Holy Father to call for us to look a little closer at the source of our priestly spirituality and fidelity. He is slowly leading us to where priestly spirituality lies. If the Instruction for Priestly Formation were to be revisited, we would find: "Without spiritual formation, pastoral formation would be left without foundation.... Spiritual formation is an extremely important element of a priest's education" (PDV 45). Aware of the history of the Church and the recurring need for the reform and renewal of priests, the Supreme Pontiff invites us to give thought to the theme: "Fidelity of Christ, Fidelity of the Priest."

As the priest, so is the Church. Historically, the biggest changes in the Church came through the reform of her clergy. The Cluniac reform, the rise of the mendicant orders and their reforms (Francis and Dominic, Carmelites Teresa and John) and the counter-Reformation orders (Jesuits, Vincentians, etc.)—all of these are reforms of the clergy that set the renewal of the Church. Now we ask: shall it be thought that a post-Vatican II renewal is so complete and all-embracing that clerical reform should be considered superfluous? If it is considered in this manner (that post-Vatican II renewal should *not* follow the past reforms of the clergy of the Church), then the recent exposés of priests' sexual abuses, misbehaviors, and the many forms of priestly impropriety here and elsewhere in the world say differently.

The truth is still equivalent to this adage: *"Talis sacerdos, qualis ecclesia."* Church renewal was always linked with clerical reform, e.g. the Tridentine reform is closely linked to the reform of priestly formation in the founding of the seminaries. It is not then an optative of the Second Vatican Council to insert a quietly hidden wish in the opening statement of *Optatam Totius* that declares: "This Council is fully aware that the desired renewal of the entire Church depends in great part upon a priestly ministry animated by the spirit of Christ" (OT 1). The life of the Church is deeply, essentially, and critically linked to the life and ministry of the priest. And, it is worth affirming the critical importance of priestly training. The relationship of dependency between the Church and the priest is here made obvious—not just as a wish alone, but as the history of the Church has proven.

Now we understand why the Pope declared 2009-2010 as the Year of the Priest. He told the plenary assembly of the Congregation for the Clergy: "Precisely to encourage priests in this striving for spiritual perfection on which, above all, the effectiveness of their ministry depends, I have decided to establish a special 'Year for Priests' that will begin on 19 June this year and last until 19 June 2010. In fact, it is the 150th anniversary of the death of the Holy Curé d'Ars, John Mary

Vianney, a true example of a pastor at the service of Christ's flock. It will be the task of your Congregation, in agreement with the diocesan Ordinaries and with the superiors of religious institutes to promote and to coordinate the various spiritual and pastoral initiatives that seem useful for making the importance of the priest's role and mission in the Church and in contemporary society ever more clearly perceived."

And so today, after we listen to reflections on the Word of God in Revelation, Church, and Mission, maybe other reflections will follow to focus on how the *Verbum* touches the *caro* of the priest. If so, then the heart of priestly spirituality shall at last be touched, and through renewal, it will then be addressed as it happened in the history of the Church.

It is not discouraging—not even shameful—to admit that up to now the *Verbum* is still scouting for a home in a *caro*. Not one that is perfect, but one that would welcome the *Verbum*, given the difficulties, the doubts, and even the failures. Brothers and sisters, we are beginning only to see the start of a renewal in the life of the Church. We are in that stage right now. My dear lay brothers and sisters, seminarians and religious, please understand that we, your priests, need your prayers. Please include us in your prayers. All of this is meant to lead us to Christ.

Salamat po sa inyong lahat.

Gaudencio Cardinal Rosales, DD, current archbishop of Manila, is also president of the CBCP Episcopal Commission on the Clergy and a member of the Congregation for the Clergy in Rome.

Academic Excellence in Ministerial Priesthood and Pastoral Work

Bienvenido F. Nebres

In the Gospel of Luke, we learn: "To whom much is given, much is also demanded" (Luke 12:48). I thought we could turn that around and say, "From whom much is demanded, we pray that much is also given." And, I like to believe that of you, future priests, bishops, and pastoral workers, much will be demanded. In this country where the faith is so strong, you are expected—whether you like it or not—to be leaders. In the disasters and challenges that face us, you will be asked to lead. And so, the question that we ask you is how you might prepare in order to be able to respond to the great challenges that will be presented to you.

Let me begin by connecting this topic with the focus of this forum: *Verbum Dei*, the Word of God. The Word, of course, is the Scripture, the written Word, the Word coming from above. But above all, it is Jesus Christ, the living Word, and his continuing ministry through the Church and the Holy Spirit in our very real and concrete world. This living Word is not up there. It is inserted, through the Incarnation, into real life and challenges as one of the gifts and capabilities of the very human communities that compose our Church and the world around us. It is in this context that I hope to share a few thoughts with you on academic excellence.

In his book entitled *Five Minds for the Future*, Howard Gardner says that the two most important intelligences are the theoretical-analytical intelligence and the practical-synthetic intelligence. The first analyzes and understands the "what" and "why" of things, which is usually what we study in philosophy or theology. The second focuses more on the "how to," on the problems, challenges, and solutions. This second intelligence is what I actually focus on.

Let me begin with real leadership and service situations where you will be asked to respond and, often, to lead. I will be using examples from here in Ateneo de Manila, but I am sure they are replicated in other places. There is much to learn from the very real things going on around us. From this we may ask questions like the following: What skills do I need to develop? What do I need to learn? What are the opportunities I need to learn these skills?

Let me begin with a challenge we face right now. I have just come from our College Covered Courts. We have been doing relief operations for the calamity victims since Saturday evening last week. To understand what we are doing there and to have a framework to respond to the kinds of challenges such as these, let me quote from a letter that I wrote to a friend in Germany, who does fundraising for our work in *Gawad Kalinga* [a community development foundation launched by the lay movement Couples for Christ]. He e-mailed me last week because he would like to do fundraising for Ondoy victims. He asked me to write something about what we are doing so he can be concrete with his appeal; I wrote:

> Dear Peter, Thank you so much for your e-mail. Yes, we need all the help we can get for the victims of the latest typhoon. I have seen several major disasters in our disaster-prone country, but this is the most devastating. It really is. The scale

is so far above what we have experienced before. *Gawad Kalinga* [GK] is at the forefront of the work for relief. GK-Ateneo is a major center of the operations, so we would be happy for any funds that would be given for this work.

So what are we doing here in Ateneo de Manila and GK-Ateneo? I would divide the process into three stages. *Stage 1:* Since Saturday, September 26, when the typhoon struck, we started monitoring the situation to see how to help. Our main concern was to keep the people we are in touch with safe. We have a permanent disaster response and management group at the Ateneo that is able to mobilize immediately. They call themselves a very nice name: DREAM Team— Disaster Response and Management Team. By Saturday night, they were already organizing, and early Sunday morning, they began to mobilize. By late morning, relief goods started to pour in, and they started distributing relief packs in the afternoon and evening of Sunday. I actually went with the group to one site, Urban Bliss, and distributed 2,000 food packs and several boxes of clothes and blankets.

I cite this for you to show you the organization. It was very organized. The goods were properly packed. An advance team went there to work with the *barangay* captain who distributed food stubs to the people and lined them up. Without these steps, it would be chaos.

This first stage of relief operations has been ongoing since Sunday and has been the major focus of our work. About two thousand students, alumni, parents, friends, and charity volunteers are working in three shifts from six in the morning until midnight. We have been delivering 15,000 to 20,000 relief packs a day to various sites.

Stage 2 is clean-up. We also started organizing volunteer groups for the clean-up of the one-foot-or-more-thick mud and debris that are in the affected areas. We started with our own Ateneo Housing for our faculty and staff the other Sunday. This is more complicated. We needed equipment, so we got a truck and a pay-loader to load the mud and the debris. We also started doing this for Provident Village.

Stage 3 is rehabilitation. This is the most complex and we are able only to start this for our own communities. Many of our students and employees are also affected. We are now doing an inventory of affected families among our employees and students. Some have lost everything. Others have lost appliances.

Our psychology and counselling departments also began to organize trauma counselling. Many are still in shock. They have lost people they know and loved. Some lost possessions that are important to them: cars, computers, books, clothes, etc., which they have worked hard for so many years and with which they earn a living. The way they expressed it is like this: "Ten, twenty years of my life are gone." Stages 1 and 2 may last for a month or so, but Stage 3 and trauma counselling will have to go on for a year or two.

Why am I citing this for you? As priests and pastoral workers, you will be faced with disasters because our country is so disaster-prone. You will be tasked to lead and to organize. There are many things one has to learn in terms of organization. Whether it is in the relief stage, clean-up stage, or rebuilding stage, you cannot just wing it. You have to have a system. And whether you like it or not, as future priests or pastoral workers, you will be asked to lead. Or if you will not be asked to lead, you should at least know how to find a good leader. You should at least know the skills needed in your community. Know that you will need organizational skills, fundraising skills, networking skills, etc. You should know the various resources that will be needed. You may not have these skills, but you should know the many people in your community who have them and know how to work with them and organize them. You may say: "This is not what I was trained for." But, we cannot choose what we are asked for; people will come to us and ask us.

Trauma counselling is one of the most difficult. If you meet with the storm victims, they are still in shock. They are still in a stage of denial. They are still hoping that something will happen so that things will come back to them. They are still trying to save everything in their house, and it is very difficult for them to let go. It is actually a form of dying. It is in the area of trauma counselling that you might not be experts, but one thing I would advise is this. There is a book of a famous writer Elizabeth Kübler-Ross entitled *On Death and Dying* where she speaks of the stages of denial, anger, bargaining, depression, and acceptance. These are not theoretical; she observed this after twenty years of working with terminally-ill cancer patients in Chicago. There is a science to this; it is well-studied and documented. I would make this book required reading and reflection for every priest and pastoral worker; for whether you like it or not, consoling and helping people become free is one of our major tasks.

Maybe just as an example: I remember four or five years ago, there was a great flood in San Francisco del Monte.

A car was swept into the creek. A mother and her two-year-old daughter were swept out of the window. She was holding her baby, but the current was so strong, she could not hang on to her child. And there I was in the wake of this two-year-old girl—their only child—and you can imagine the loss. What do you say? What I learned from Kübler-Ross is this: that in the end, there is only one mission in life and that is to learn how to love and teach others how to love. And so, I told the mother and father, "Your little two-year-old girl certainly loved you and maybe her mission for you was to teach you how to love. And you have grown in love, because she was with you these two years. Maybe that was God's mission for her." When I went back for the funeral mass, the mother approached me and said, "Yes, she taught us how to love."

I also sometimes use the image of the two disciples walking to Emmaus for many difficult times. If you analyze that story, the two disciples were also undergoing these stages of denial, anger, bargaining, and depression. And so, I tell people: "You will go through these stages. You cannot avoid it. You will go through denial, anger, bargaining, depression and so on. It is OK. Jesus accepted that with his disciples, but I hope that He will walk with you." If there is one area that you have to learn in a situation like this—because clearly you will be asked to do this—it would be how to deal with people who go through a form of dying.

There are others that I could speak about to you. You could learn a lot if you prepare for the next elections—especially on how to organize. So much of the talk about the next elections is about blaming one another. But, whether we like it or not, they will come and the key is to organize for it. Encourage people to go out and register. Learn the new way of poll watching, because it will be different from before; there are new skills that will be needed. So, if you want to have better leaders, you will have to do that.

The last area is poverty. How do we deal with poverty? We have been working with the poverty problem for so long; so, let me cite some relatively successful examples and the challenges they present to us.

The most dramatic of course is *Gawad Kalinga,* the most extensive movement to build housing, communities, and families of the poor. What I want to tell you, leaders of the Church, are the challenges that are presented to us. First, there is the ecclesiological and missiological challenge. You can see this in the debates among the bishops in the Philippines on how *Gawad Kalinga* (GK) and Couples for Christ (CFC) should relate with non-Catholic groups. What happened to Father Murray during Vatican II is basically the same debate found in the work of GK: What is our understanding of the Church? Is the Church a closed fortress or is she open to the world? What are CFC and GK as Catholic movements? Are they to stay *intra*-Church? How will they relate to the Born Again groups, to the Mormons, to the Muslims? This issue on the work of GK and CFC is not different than the debate of Vatican II.

How we prosper in the future, and whether we will really be a Church serving all the poor—regardless of faith—in this country will depend on how we resolve this debate. This is a very difficult challenge for me as I speak to different groups, because so many different arguments are embedded in very different ecclesiologies. And so, this is a challenge of academic excellence for you. You have to go back to the debates of the Judaic Church encountering the Greco-Roman world. You have to go back to the debates during the Council of Jerusalem—whether Christianity would remain a sect or become a world religion. It is not new; it is an old challenge which has to be faced today.

On the level of spirituality, we are also challenged in

working with others. How do you understand discernment? In a lot of my own discussions with my colleagues in CFC and GK, discernment for them is completely "from above." Leaders discern and the people below obey. But, discernment is deeper than that. Discernment is also "listening to the ground"; it means listening to the reality. It is like Peter being confronted by Paul and Barnabas about the reality of the Greek and Roman world, and being challenged in his own beliefs on what the Church should be. In this movement, which is clearly and simply a work for the poor, you begin to find out that, because it is so great and so extensive, it demands academic excellence. You have to understand your Church history. You have to understand how the Church has grown encountering these things in the past. Help others to understand how the Church today addresses this new challenge of the world.

There is also the challenge in organization. The challenge too in my work with both CFC and GK is that they are also human organizations which have become very large. We are doing an organizational development study of GK and helping them understand that they are like a family business that has become very big. Actually, what they are going through is very typical of family businesses that have become very successful and now need to professionalize—a very similar challenge.

I just gave these to you as examples of the kinds of things that you will face. And, you must understand these challenges. What are all these leading to? Much of our education in the seminaries is about philosophy and theology. This is important of course. We must understand our tradition, our legacy. We must understand the Word handed down to us and pass it on in fidelity. But, we must also, in the end, bring it down and "incarnate" it in the lives of people. I know that you do a lot of apostolates and my question to you is: How organized are you? How much do you reflect on these apostolates? How much do you reflect on whether you are really addressing peoples' needs? Do you measure? Are you learning? Are you discovering the skills you need in the future?

A young woman whom I admire a lot, Melissa Yeung, graduated from Ateneo in Development Studies in 2007. She really wanted to dedicate herself to working for indigenous peoples (IPs), so she was there in Bukidnon working for the Talaandigs and others. A big famine happened, and she realized that people were hungry and that she could not really help them. We had a very long talk, and we agreed that she will take a Masters course in Entrepreneurship. She has done that and she was very good at it. Now, she is running a lot of social entrepreneurship programs for IPs in Mindanao. She understood the need. She realized that with her own skills she could not do it. She saw what she needed and the things that existed out there, and she addressed them. That is what I would really say to you. Look around. Look at the skills you have. Look for where you can gain the skills and impart them to others.

The Word of God comes to us in the Scriptures, philosophy, and theology. But, the Scriptures, philosophy, and theology have to be read and understood in the real life context of the community and the people to whom we must minister. The Word of God is a living Word because it takes on its meaning today in the very particular context of our people. It is "incarnated." We must learn how to read this real life context, how to learn from it, and how to work with it. This is not to tell you, of course, that you should learn many things, that you should learn science and technology, business and psychology (although they would be helpful). But, what I am telling you is that you should draw from the opportunities that are available to you, observe the skills and the academic learning that make them succeed, and learn much. And maybe, to be humble, to find out that there are many lay people in your community who know a lot more than you. And, one of the gifts you should have is to know who they are, and how to harness their skills.

A lot of academic excellence is theoretical and analytical. We learn that in our philosophy and theology. But, there is also much that we have to learn in the synthetic and the practical, and this is the world of business, management, and engineering. You may not take business or management courses, but you should know the people in your community who have these skills. Bring them in and listen to them. Do not theologize immediately. Try to see what they can contribute to you. Learn from experience. In my own life, I would say, I have had a lot of theoretical things; but in the end, the most important learning you have is gained from reflecting from real life experience, drawing from it, and learning what you can do or cannot do and move on from there.

Our challenge as priests and pastoral workers in our country is immense, because, firstly, the needs are so great—there are so many poor and we are so disaster-prone. Secondly, whether we like it or not, we will be tasked with leadership and so many things will be asked of us. I hope that all these disasters and the responses to them have become learning opportunities. Typhoons Ondoy and Pepeng—they can be for us a teaching moment, a learning moment. As you move on, later on in your ministry, you might go back to this experience and say, "Yes, we learned a lot from this experience. We can now move on and do more for all the other challenges that will face us in the future."

Congratulations again on this forum and thank you very much. May we all give our very best to the great needs that surround us today.

Bienvenido F. Nebres, SJ is the current President of the Ateneo de Manila University.

Encountering God through Words

Victor C. de Jesus

From early this morning, we have heard many, many words. Bishop Bacani spoke of how a Buddhist once complained, upon reading the Bible, that our God is a rather *wordy* god, perhaps even a noisy god. But, have you ever wondered how it is to be in a world without words? I am not asking if you have ever been deaf or mute, because you can be a deaf-mute but still live in the world of language, of sign language at least. Our bishop [Honesto Ongtioco] here knows sign language. And, signs *are* words. So, have you ever lived in a world without words?

Well, all of us should be able to answer "Yes"! All of us have lived in a world without words, at least for a time. But precisely because it was a world without words, maybe it is hard to remember. What I refer to is the time when we were infants. The roots of the word "infant" precisely refer to someone who cannot speak, cannot produce words. The infant is confined to a very limited and a very narrow world— what the philosopher Bernard Lonergan calls the "world of the immediate," the "world of immediacy," the "world of already-out-there-right-now." What the infant can see, touch, hear, feel—that is what is real for him, the world of the immediate. Nothing else exists; nothing else is real, except what is immediate to me, the infant.

The world of immediacy is a world of reality, but a

very limited part of reality. Why? Because the infant has not crossed the bridge from the world without words, to the wide, wild, and wonderful world of words—the world of meaning or, more precisely, the world mediated by meaning.

Father Arévalo told us earlier that part of the Bible's mission, in a sense, is to excite that question within us: what is the meaning of life? And, in a sense, there is only one word that answers that question. And, His name is Jesus. But let me return for a moment to a consideration of the world mediated by meaning.

The world of meaning is such a great gift of God to us— the world mediated by words. It is also a *world* therefore, like the world of the immediate. And, it too is a world of reality. But, unlike the world of immediacy, the world mediated by meaning is a world of deeper and more exalted realties, many of them unseen. In the world mediated by meaning, there are realities that are beyond what we can immediately see, hear, feel, or touch. And these are realities that, even if we do not see them, are real, nevertheless. Think of the words "freedom," "sacrifice," or "self-denial." These are things the infant cannot understand until he crosses over on the bridge of words into the world mediated by meaning, the world *bridged* by words of meaning.

Father Nebres said earlier we should all read Elizabeth Kübler-Ross' *On Death and Dying*. There is a movie that perhaps I might strongly recommend—*The Miracle Worker*. It is a very touching film about Helen Keller [though the title actually refers to her teacher, Annie Sullivan]. Do you remember Helen Keller? Because of an early illness, she became deaf and blind, and therefore, effectively also mute. She never got to hear or understand a spoken word.

So she was locked in the world of immediacy. And

her family and herself had tremendous difficulty trying to fit her into their world. For example, when she would eat, of course, she had no concept of manners. Even if there were guests, she would basically feel around for any plates beside her and in front of her, grab the food, and stuff it into her mouth. Of course, she could not learn from example, because as a blind and deaf person, she could not see how others eat nor could anybody speak to her about it. It was *painful* for her. She would feel a slap on her hand and she could not understand why. She could not understand exactly what was going on. She could not hear their words; she could not see their reactions to her behavior.

But of course, she was in the world of immediacy and she did not know any better. She was trapped … until that wonderful time when Annie Sullivan came into her life. Annie would do the sign language alphabet into Helen's palm; and using various techniques, she established some types of communication between Helen and herself. But for a long time, it all seemed useless.

One day, even Annie lost her patience as a teacher. She was trying to get Helen to eat in the conventional way. But, by this time, Helen was becoming impatient with the tugging and with the various stimuli that were being sent her way and she started thrashing about. Then Helen threw a whole pitcher of water into Annie's face [at least, that is the way the movie shows us]. And Annie in a fit of impatience dragged Helen with the pitcher out into the yard where there was a water pump. She thrust Helen's hand under the stream of the pump and on the palm of Helen's other hand, Annie kept signing "W-A-T-E-R," "W-A-T-E-R," "W-A-T-E-R."

Then, all of a sudden, Helen's face changes! She is *free*! She has discovered … the *WORD*! She discovered the bridge, the connection between these sensations made by the sign language on her palm and the world of meaning. She discovered the wonderful thing that, in our First Reading, Adam gave to the animals. He gave them ... *names* (Gen 2:19). And it finally dawns on Helen that there is such a thing as signs, letters, words, names, language. Her face lights up and peace descends ... and she is healed.

Then, Helen looks for Annie her teacher and she pulls Annie, by smell I suppose, she goes to her mother and then gestures into Annie's hand as if to say, "Name this. Name this! Name this wonderful, soft, embracing thing. Give me its name." And Annie spelled it into Helen's hands: "M-O-T-H-E-R." Then, bounding from one place to another, Helen pulled Annie along with her asking Annie about everything around her that could be named. Finally, Helen taps on the chest of Annie and wordlessly asks Annie to name herself. And, Annie signs into Helen's hand: "T-E-A-C-H-E-R."

This beautiful day, we have been celebrating the Word of God, and I am very, very moved because this was our seminarians' initiative. They basically "importuned" our three Bishops to speak to us [and now Bishop Ongtioco who leads us in prayer]. The seminarians asked our three great bishop-*teachers*, all alumni of San Jose Seminary, to speak to us today. They also got Father Catalino Arévalo to come and speak to us. Father Arévalo was the teacher of Bishops Bacani, Tagle, and David while Bishop Bacani himself in turn was also the teacher of Bishops Tagle and David. We have been so blessed by the words of these teachers. They have reminded us of how the Word of God has a voice, has a face, has a home, and has roads upon which we must travel! And I say, "Praise the Lord and thank you dear Bishops for all of this."

The Gospel today is a reminder of another special word to us—"marriage." Marriage yields the "domestic church," as it were, the first home of the Word. Marriage— the community of a Christian husband and wife who, by their giving of their *words* to each other, image for us—with a voice, with faces, with a home, and with the roads that they also tread—Christ's own *word* of love, His loving commitment to His Bride, the Church.

At the beginning of this homily, I spent quite a bit of time discussing the world of meaning, because, again, there is a reality in the world of meaning that in the world of immediacy is senseless. The word "promise," how could you have explained that to Hellen Keller before she discovered the "word"? And how do we explain to Helen Keller before she was healed, before she discovered language, how God is a *promising* God? He has a promising future for us, and one of the key ways by which he reveals this to us is by the sacrament of marriage. The giving and keeping of the word that couples struggle to do in their marriage strengthens all of us by being signs of Christ's own love for all of us. A love that those of us here who are religious and those of us called to celibacy are also fed by that word of the lives of you married couples.

Some of us, of course, have experienced the pain of estrangement, the pain of the breaking of the words of commitment given in marriage. But in the end, our truest spouse is God who became Word in Jesus and tells us, "I shall be your Spouse. I shall be Word made flesh for you. I shall be Word to nourish you with fire. I shall be Bread for your journey." God gives us His very Word—in flesh, in sacrament and sign—the One whom we celebrate and praise this afternoon. God gives His Word and keeps it, in spite of our own breaking of *our* word.

We turn to God now and we give our word again. The Synod reminds us that the Word is the very *heart* of God. He invites us, into whose hearts he poured his Spirit, so that we may call him *"Abba."* We are invited to give our word again, to renew our commitment at the table of the Covenant, the *New* Covenant. And so, we ask that we may keep our word to the One who keeps us.

May the Lord bless and keep us—keep us faithful to the Word, to the marriage covenant, and, nourished by the Word, on fire for the Word that we may again *sing* of the Word of God and proclaim His praise. Amen.

Victor C. de Jesus, SJ is currently the Rector of San Jose Major Seminary and a faculty member of Loyola School of Theology.

The *Verbum Dei* Story

Sir-lien Hugh Tadeo

This book of reflections on the Word of God would be somewhat incomplete, if the story behind its evolution were not told—even if very briefly. On August 25, 2009, after the evening recreation time at San Jose Seminary, Mark Reyes, chairman of the academic committee, mentioned that Imus Bishop Luis A. Tagle was unable to be present at a previously scheduled academic forum with our seminary community. Immediately, Mark and I tried to think of an alternative; Bishop Pablo David of San Fernando, Pampanga came to mind as a possible replacement. However, it was already too late to ask him to fill in the schedule planned with Bishop Tagle. Mark then presented the idea of having the academic forum open to all the students of the Loyola School of Theology. I readily agreed, but I also thought of organizing a larger endeavor that would showcase *Josefino* minds and talents. At the same time that this discussion unfolded, a campaign was underway to raise funds for the *Bukluran* Inter-College Seminary Meet being hosted by San Jose Seminary in November. So, we thought of launching a whole day forum which would feature the illustrious alumni of San Jose—and hopefully help underwrite some *Bukluran* expenses.

Josefino bishops Luis Tagle, Pablo David and Teodoro Bacani were the obvious choices. Immediately, I sent Bishops David and Bacani a text message regarding the proposed project. Initially, they were invited to present their doctoral dissertations, but Bishop "Ambo" David reacted instantly against the idea; as an alternative possibility, he suggested that they give the talks he and Bishop Chito delivered during the CBCP plenary assembly about the Word of God. Since the response from all three bishops seemed positive after only twenty minutes of speculating, the academic committee approached our seminary rector Father Victor de Jesus, SJ and presented to him what we proposed. We decided to the dub the event: *Josefino Forum: Verbum Dei: Reflections on the Word of God*.

Within one month, the schedule was in place, promotional materials were released to parishes, and invitation letters were sent to schools, seminaries, benefactors, and friends. Father Catalino G. Arévalo, SJ agreed to participate with a final synthesis of the talks of his three bishop-students. Manila Archbishop Gaudencio Cardinal Rosales graciously adjusted his schedule to present the opening remarks. Cubao Bishop Honesto Ongtioco happily accepted to preside at a final mass. Ateneo de Manila University President Father Bienvenido Nebres, SJ agreed to give an exhortation on academic excellence in line with Ateneo's sesquicentennial celebration; in addition, his office enabled the use of the Irwin Theater at a discounted rate. *Hangad* lovingly volunteered to provide some inspirational music. The Assisi Development Foundation and our *Josefino* alumni Monsignor Daniel Sta. Maria and Father Benito Tuazon generously contributed some funds to allay operation and promotion expenses.

During the last week of September 2009, two powerful typhoons struck the country, leaving unprecedented massive damage in parts of Metro Manila and Luzon; we feared only few would be able to attend the Forum. Despite these obstacles, we firmly resolved to continue on the scheduled date. By God's gracious providence, the forum became a major success! Truly, the word of God must be preached whether in or out of season … *insta opportune, importune* (2 Tim. 4:2).

After the forum itself, San Jose alumnus Father James Kroeger, MM encouraged us to publish the rich presentations in *Insta*, our alumni magazine. Initially, we thought of employing the usual format of *Insta*. However, all soon realized it would be a genuine service to the wider Church in the Philippines, if the material were co-published as a book with Jesuit Communications and Claretian Publications. Joseph Zaldivar, *Insta* editor, and I prepared and edited the transcripts. *Insta* staff members Edmel Raagas, Regin Tenorio, and Julius Habana designed the cover and prepared some additional artwork; Mark Purugganan would assist with the finances and circulation. With constant editorial assistance from Father Kroeger throughout the whole process, all our efforts have resulted in this volume you now hold in your hands.

Indeed, what started as a spark of inspiration in two seminarians resulted in setting us ablaze; the fiery flame reached our seminary community as well as the receptive audience we gathered on October 4, 2009. A burning passion for the Word of God was enkindled and spread effectively. What was originally intended to be an hour of reflection among some seminarians became a day of fire shared with the larger community. What appeared to be an impulsive decision was God's grace after all. Together with the staff of *Insta*, we sincerely hope that through this book, that flame of love for the Word, effectively kindled in us during the *Verbum Dei* Forum, will remain as an enduring ember within; may that same Word burn in us and shine forth from us!

Sir-lien Hugh Tadeo, a seminarian of the Diocese of Cubao and *Insta* associate editor, studies at Loyola School of Theology and resides in San Jose Seminary.

GO OUT
TO THE WHOLE
WORLD,
PROCLAIM
THE GOOD NEWS
TO ALL
CREATION